Understanding and Implementing Inclusion:

A Practical Guide for Classroom Teachers

Understanding and Implementing Inclusion:

A Practical Guide for Classroom Teachers

Elaine Francis

Ruth M. Joseph

Anne M. Howard

Christopher-Gordon Publishers, Inc.
Norwood, Massachusetts

Copyright Acknowledgments

Every effort has been made to contact copyright holders for permission to reproduce borrowed material where necessary. We apologize for any oversights and would be happy to rectify them in future printings.

Excerpt from Lipsky & Gartner, In William Stainback & Susan Stainback (eds.) "Inclusive Education And School Restructuring" In *Controversial Issues Confronting Special Education*: Published by Allyn and Bacon, Boston, MA. Copyright © 1996 by Pearson Education. Adapted by permission of the publisher.

Excerpt from Warger, C. *Five homework strategies for teaching students with disabilities*. Retrieved January 4, 2002 from http://ericec.org/digests/e608.html. Reprinted with permission of the ERIC Clearinghouse on Disabilities and Gifted Education, a division of The Council for Exceptional Children, Arlington, VA. Copyright © 2001.

Excerpt from Whitten, E. & Dieker, L. Intervention assistance teams: A broader view [Electronic Version Retrieved June 16, 2001]. *Preventing School Failure*, 95(40), 41-45. Reprinted with permission of the Helen Dwight Reid Educational Foundation. Published by Heldref Publications, 1319 18th Street, NW, Washington, DC 20036-1802. www.heldref.org. Copyright © 1995.

The Snapshot IEP adapted from Goor, M., & McCoy, E. (1993). Presented at TASH: The Association for Persons with Severe Handicaps, Baltimore, MD. Reprinted with permission.

Christopher~Gordon Publishers, Inc.
Bridging Theory and Practice
1502 Providence Highway, Suite #12
Norwood, Massachusetts 02062
800-934-8322
781-762-5577

Printed in the United State of America
10 9 8 7 6 5 4 3 2 1   08 07 06 05 04

ISBN: 1-929024-64-9
Library of Congress Catalogue Number: 2003109003

Dedication

For our parents:

those who are with us

and those who are not

Table of Contents

Preface

We designed this book for general education teachers and administrators who have limited experience with students who have special needs, or who wish to learn more about "inclusion." We begin with a historical perspective, tracing the development of the current educational system for students with special needs. We attempted to give the reader an opportunity to understand the complex system that was developed to include separate facilities and classes for students with disabilities. We try to convey that it is difficult to promote a new service system when it will require the dismantling of the old way of doing things.

Once the historical development of exclusionary practices is presented, we set forth the argument that these practices are both unconstitutional and unethical in an educational model. The emergence of "mainstreaming," "integration," and "inclusion" as terms for addressing the needs of all students is examined. The definition as well as the pros and cons of each approach are discussed. We argue that inclusionary practices are those that accept all children as the responsibility of everyone in the educational community and is *the* most effective way of teaching all children.

We have tried to keep the book general in the sense that it does not provide detailed "how to" recipes for creating inclusionary environments. Rather, we present a philosophy, a way of thinking about inclusion, that drives appropriate practice. The methodology for inclusion that is presented in this text is at a global level; however, additional resources and references for further information on this topic are listed at the end of each chapter.

We examine the need for systemic change and consider ways to address this change. Links between educational reform and inclusion are forged, and the reader is presented with very obvious arguments—and our belief—that the goals of the educational system are the goals for all students; thus inclusion should be our way of practice.

Programmatic changes that promote inclusion are also presented in a global way. We provide the reader with a structure for thinking about ways in which a student's Individual Education Plan (IEP) is at the heart of effective teaching in any setting. Broad suggestions for thinking about how we believe a student's day could be structured are presented. Research on best practices of teaching, e.g., cooperative learning, multiple intelligence practices, etc., are summarized.

In the final chapter, we ask readers to think about ways in which they can promote inclusionary practices in their school. We encourage them to set small, achievable goals that, when attained, will serve as models for others in their building and district.

Introduction

The question of where to educate children with disabilities is not a new one. It has been more than 25 years since the passage of Public Law (PL) 94-142, the landmark legislation guaranteeing all children—no matter how severe their disabilities—a free and appropriate public education. Most school districts continue to grapple with the fundamental question of how best to organize and provide special education services. With the passage of time, however, has come the realization that *including* students with disabilities is preferable to segregating or excluding them. Yet the shift toward more inclusive educational practices has been uneven, and the implementation of inclusive practices has taken many forms. In some schools inclusion has resulted in the closing down of all special education classes and the placement of students with disabilities in the general education classroom 100% of the time. Other schools have chosen to redesign special education classes so that general and special education teachers coteach classes of students with and without disabilities. And still other school communities have redeployed some or all of their special education resources into support services, which are available to all students. The various models that have been utilized are endless.

The goal of this book is to help beginning general education teachers to work more successfully in whatever inclusion model they encounter. Given the diversity of practice, it is impossible to describe for beginning general education teachers exactly what inclusion is, or what it might look like in their first teaching position. In chapter 1, however, we attempt to describe some of the more common meanings of the term "inclusion" and the related terms "integration" and "mainstreaming." Various models of inclusion are considered, and the origins of the shift toward inclusive practices are examined.

Not surprisingly, inclusion is a controversial topic. Chapter 2 addresses the nature of the controversy by examining the views of various constituents in schools and communities. It is our belief that understanding the perspectives of others will help us to work together in creating a successful school experience for all children.

Throughout this book, we stress the fact that inclusion is more than a set of strategies or techniques; inclusion is a *philosophy* about how we believe children should learn. Chapters 3 and 4 provide an overview of this philosophy and some examples of the tools needed to implement it effectively. Chapter 3 looks at curriculum and ways that it can be modified so that all children can have access to a common curriculum, even if their learning objectives are different. Chapter 4 provides some of the essential strategies teachers can use in the classroom to ensure that all children will learn. In chapter 5, we examine how a student's Individualized Educational Program (IEP) can serve as a guide to ensure that the child has the services and support he or she needs to access the general education. For the beginning general education teacher, a well-written IEP can provide the essential information and tools necessary to address that student's needs within the general education classroom.

Despite the fact that inclusion is an initiative that has been mandated by law and has been implemented in many forms over the past few decades, there are many parents, professionals, and students who resist this model for various reasons. Chapter 5 presents suggestions for how various constituents in schools can advocate to make the philosophy of inclusion a reality in their school.

While this text presents some beginning steps in thinking about and implementing inclusionary practices, it is not meant to provide every answer. Suggested readings will assist those who need and/or are interested in pursuing this topic further. We encourage readers to consider our thoughts, ideas, and the research we present, and to use this to make their school a better place where all children are welcomed as part of a school family.

Understanding Inclusion

What Is Inclusion?

What is inclusion?

Inclusion is a term for which there is no universally accepted definition, and there is no one model of inclusion. Visit five inclusive classrooms, and you are likely to see five different ways of including students with various disabilities. The terms *mainstreaming* and *integration* are often used interchangeably with inclusion. Although there is not an agreed-upon term or common definition of inclusion, a distinction can be made between these three terms. Joy Rogers (1993) has proposed the following definition of mainstreaming:

> …the selective placement of special education students in one or more regular education classes. Mainstreaming proponents generally assume that a student must "earn" his or her opportunity to be mainstreamed through the ability to "keep up with" the work generally assigned by the teacher to other students in the class. This concept is closely linked to traditional forms of special education service delivery (Rogers, 1993, p. 4).

For example, a student may spend time in a resource room to receive specialized instruction in an effort to prepare the student for reentry, or "mainstreaming," back into the general education classroom. Sometimes referred to as the "readiness model," the premise is that the student begins and receives instruction outside of the general education classroom until he or she "catches up" with the "typical" students. Years of this type of instruction have proved ineffective.

Mainstreamed students are typically included in the regular classroom for nonacademic subjects, such as art and music. The two groups of students may be seen as quite different in their abilities and needs, but the benefits of bringing the two groups together are recognized. Figure 1.1 illustrates the separateness, as well as the overlap, in a school program employing mainstreaming for students with disabilities.

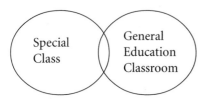

Figure 1.1 Mainstreaming illustrates a very separate view of the two groups of students, the curriculum they require, and the responsibilities of the staff, yet it recognizes the need to bring the students together.

Integration is seen as the bringing together of students with and without disabilities. Integration suggests that students come together for nonacademic subjects as well as for academic subjects. It recognizes that students with disabilities can benefit from access to the general education curriculum. The two groups, however, continue to be seen as distinctly different, and students with disabilities are not yet viewed as full participating members of the school community. Special educators maintain responsibility for their students and general education faculty see their role as working with "typical students" only. Figure 1.2 illustrates integration.

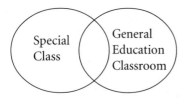

Figure 1.2 Integration: the two groups of students are seen as different, but are brought together frequently during the school day.

Inclusion, on the other hand, is the welcoming of all students into the total life of the school community (curriculum, environment, social events, and self-concept of the school), regardless of their disabilities. Students with disabilities begin in the general education classroom and are part of the group. They belong to this group and are only removed from the class for instruction when, even after extensive accommodations and adaptations, their educational needs cannot be met in the general education classroom.

For example, a high school student with disabilities would begin the school day in a homeroom with nondisabled peers. He or she would follow an individualized schedule accessing the general education curriculum and classes when appropriate and would only receive instruction outside the general education classroom when class activities are determined to be inadequate to meet the student's needs.

Figure 1.3 Illustrates inclusion as full acceptance of all students as members of the school community, with no distinction between each group.

Pearpoint & Forest (Stainback & Stainback, 1992) provide a descriptive definition of inclusion:

> Inclusion means welcoming everyone—all students, all citizens—back into our schools and communities. Our schools should be communities where all students are thought of as gifted, communities where all students are welcomed and accepted for their exceptional learning needs. Inclusion can be thought of as the new *ABCs*—acceptance, belonging, and community. Our schools should be safe and caring communities that value, respect, and celebrate differences (Stainback & Stainback, 1992, pp. xv–xvi).

Inclusion, in the purest form, is a sense of belonging. We all want to belong to or feel membership with some group—whether it is in our neighborhood, at work, church, or school. According to Maslow's (1968) hierarchy of needs, safety, belongingness, and self-esteem are basic needs and must be satisfied. No matter what the ability or disability of a person, educators and schools need to satisfy these basic needs.

We believe inclusion is a philosophy. It is a philosophy of how and where students with disabilities should be educated. It is the belief that all children belong in—and can learn in—the general education environment. We do not believe there is a single model or prescription for effective inclusion. There is no one right way or one best way to include students with disabilities. We do believe that all individuals have the right to become participating and contributing members of a variety of communities. For the purposes of this book, we will use the word *inclusion* to indicate a situation where students with disabilities are members of the general education classroom.

They are part of a group; they belong, and are removed from the group for instruction only when—after extensive modifications, accommodations, and adaptations have been tried—their educational needs cannot be met in the general education classroom.

Why include now?

In order to answer this question, we review the Supreme Court decision of 1954, Brown v. the Board of Education of Topeka, Kansas (Brown v. Board of Education of Topeka, 347 U.S. 483, 74 Sup. Ct. 686, 1954). A quote from this decision follows:

> In these days, it is doubtful that any child may reasonably be expected to succeed in life if he is denied the opportunity of an education. Such an opportunity, where the state has undertaken to provide it, is a right which must be made available to all on equal terms...We conclude that in the field of public education the doctrine of "separate but equal" has no place. Separate educational facilities are inherently unequal (Brown v. Board of Education, 1954, 9.493).

While this decision was written for a case dealing with racial discrimination, the basis for this discussion has influenced more recent court decisions dealing with discrimination and the separation of students with disabilities.

Another key legislative action supporting inclusion of students with disabilities is PARC v. Commonwealth of Pennsylvania (1971). The Pennsylvania Association for Retarded Citizens (PARC) brought its case before the United States District Court for the Eastern District of Pennsylvania. The case was brought forth by the parents of children who had been institutionalized with a diagnosis of mental retardation. A critical outcome of this case was the provision in the decree that placement in a regular school class is preferable to a special class (Pennsylvania Association for Retarded Citizens v. Commonwealth of Pennsylvania, 1971).

A number of similar suits followed, which ultimately contributed to the passage of Public Law (PL) 94-142, the Education of All Handicapped Children Act (EHA), in 1975. PL 94-142's major provision was the concept of "least restrictive environment." Since the passage of this law, the number of students receiving special education services has continually increased. Separate "special" education evolved as a response to the specialized learning needs of students with disabilities. A large percentage of special education services and instruction was delivered outside of the general education classroom. Resource rooms, substantially separate classrooms, and private schools were—and still are—common settings in which students with disabilities receive instruction.

Today, PL 94-142 is known as the Individuals with Disabilities Education Act (IDEA), which guarantees free appropriate public education (FAPE) to all students with disabilities in the "least restrictive environment" (LRE) to the fullest extent possible. The Individualized Educational Program (IEP), required by IDEA, ensures that students with disabilities have access to the least restrictive environment. According to IDEA, least restrictive environment means that:

> ...to the maximum extent appropriate, children with disabilities, including children in public and private institutions or other care facilities, are educated with children who do not have disabilities, and that special education classes, separate schooling, or other removal of children with disabilities from the general educational environment occurs only when the nature or severity of the disability is such that education in general classes with the use of supplementary aids and services cannot be achieved satisfactorily... (20 U.S.C., section 1412 [5][B]).

Each year, the U.S. Office of Special Education Programs (OSEP) prepares its *Annual Report to Congress on the Implementation of the Individuals with Disabilities Education Act.* The 23rd such report, released in 2001, indicated that the percentage of students (aged 6–21 years) served in general education classes has continually increased, and virtually all students (96%) are served in regular school buildings. These findings vary, however, depending on a student's disability. Students with emotional disturbance (33%), mental retardation (51%), and multiple disabilities (45%) are most likely to spend more than 60% of their school day outside a general education classroom (U.S. DOE, 2001).

Prior to the passage of IDEA, Congress passed the Rehabilitation Act of 1973, which includes Section 504. Unlike IDEA, Section 504 does not provide educational funding to states. It does, however, make it illegal for any programs receiving federal funding to discriminate against an individual on the basis of his or her disability. It guarantees basic civil rights to people with disabilities in many important aspects of society and was extended through the Americans with Disabilities Act (ADA), passed in 1990.

Section 504 provides the greatest education benefits to those students who do not qualify for IDEA services. Section 504 requires that schools and teachers provide these students with reasonable accommodations. Many children with health impairments, Attention Deficit Disorder with Hyperactivity (ADHD), Attention Deficit Disorder (ADD), or temporary physical impairments have disabilities but do not qualify for special education services under IDEA because they are making progress in school. They do, however, require accommodations, which may be made under Section 504 to meet the nondiscrimination standard.

In addition to the impact of legislative and litigated decisions moving schools closer to inclusion, professional literature and research has also played a significant role. Lipsky & Gartner (1996) cite six factors that have contributed to the movement of inclusion: 1) growing concern as to the limited outcomes for all students, particularly those in special education, 2) the broader education reform movement, which calls attention to higher standards for all students, 3) court cases that have supported inclusion, 4) insistence by the disability rights movement for full participation as well as the effects of attention to the ADA and its implementation, 5) the continuously rising costs of special education, and 6) increased parental advocacy and involvement in school reform efforts (Lipsky & Gartner, 1996).

In addition to the legal mandates and the factors cited by Lipsky & Gartner, we believe there are a number of other reasons to include students with disabilities. First of all, the regular education classroom provides chronologically age-appropriate peers. When we were in school, our circle of friends consisted of peers of our own age or very close to it. Age-appropriate peers, especially for youth, are a natural occurrence. A general education classroom of age-appropriate peers can provide an optimal environment for students with disabilities to develop social relationships. In our experience, some segregated classrooms often include students with differences in age of six years or greater. Typical 16-year-olds and typical 10-year-olds are not likely to have similar extracurricular interests, hobbies, pastimes, etc. We do them a disservice when we assume they will share common interests simply because they read or function academically at the same age level.

It is also important that the students are engaged in age-appropriate activities using age-appropriate materials. A 10-year-old student with disabilities should not be stacking rings on a pole to strengthen fine motor skills or improve finger dexterity. A typical 10-year-old would not engage in this activity. Even if a 10-year-old student is functioning at a developmental age of three, this student should be given activities that are age-appropriate, such as using a key to open a locker, using a knife and fork to eat, hanging objects on hooks, sharpening pencils, etc.

Secondly, the "best" and most appropriate models are in the general education classroom. Typical students can be strong role models for language and socially appropriate behavior and dress. If not included in the general education classroom, students with disabilities are not afforded the opportunity to learn from these role models. Segregated classrooms typically do not have strong role models for students with disabilities. In many instances, students with disabilities—when assigned to segregated settings—are grouped with individuals with "abilities" similar to theirs. For example, if a student who is nonverbal is placed in a classroom with other students who are non-verbal, when will this student have the opportunity to learn language from peer models? Likewise, if a student with behavior problems is grouped with other students with behavior problems, who will model good behavior for that student? What opportunities will there be for the former student to learn language and the latter student to learn appropriate behavior?

A third reason we believe students with disabilities should be included is that when "best" teaching practices are employed in the general education classroom to meet the needs of students with disabilities, *all* students will benefit. The use of strategies, modifications, adaptations, and accommodations do not have to be limited to students with disabilities. Students who are gifted and talented, students who are at-risk, and students who are typical may benefit from the strategies, modifications, accommodations, and adaptations provided for students with disabilities in the classroom.

Also, we believe that if a student with disabilities begins in the general education classroom and then leaves when necessary, the student is more apt to be considered a member of the classroom. If the opposite is the case, and the student begins in a segregated classroom and goes into the general education classroom for some activities, the student is more apt to be seen as a "visitor" and not a true member of the classroom. It is better to be an "insider" who goes out for short periods of time than it is to be an "outsider" who comes in (Brown, Schwarz, Udarvi-Solner, Kampschroer, Johnson, Jorgensen, & Gruenewald, 1991). Like Brown et al., we believe this to be true.

What does inclusion look like?

Picture a fourth-grade youngster, Eric, who has a significant language disability with limited expressive language and difficulty reading. He arrives at school in a small van, accompanied by a handful of other students, all of whom have significant disabilities. The van is met by a special education teacher or paraprofessional. The students are escorted off the bus and brought to their "special class," where they participate in opening exercises and begin their day. Since most of the students have language delays, the person doing most of the communicating is the teacher. During the day, at various times, students leave the special class to participate in art, gym, and/or music with their nondisabled peers. Eric leaves the special class at 10:00 a.m. and joins a general education fourth-grade class in the art room. The students in general education, who have been together since they arrived at school, glance at Eric and perhaps offer him a smile before they go on about their business. During the art class, some of the students approach Eric and talk with him, but it is clear that he is perceived primarily as a "drop in" who will return to his special class when they all move on to their math class.

Eric enjoys his visit to art class, not because he loves art, but because it gives him an opportunity to be with fellow students who communicate with him and at least acknowledge his presence. At lunch and recess he remains with his peers from the special class because this will allow the special education teacher to more closely monitor him, as he is her responsibility.

Now picture a different scenario. Eric arrives at school on the bus with his "typical peers." Along with all the other bus riders, Eric is greeted at the bus by the principal and the teacher who has bus duty. He moves to his fourth-grade class with his peers and participates with them in opening exercises. As the class moves into their language arts period, Eric begins work on the same language activities, which have been modified for him. He may also receive occasional support from a peer or paraprofessional. At lunch, Eric sits with his friends who do not have disabilities. He not only enjoys the company of his typical classmates but also learns from his models as they communicate with him and with one another.

These two scenarios present two very different days for a student with disabilities. The first scenario illustrates ways in which a model of separateness sends many messages to such students about their place in a community. It also illustrates ways in which students' opportunities for learning are limited and/or enhanced by their classmates. The second scenario illustrates the ways in which inclusion can help a student with disabilities be a member of a community and learn from the entire community.

Inclusion is a process, not a series of events during a day. These scenarios above show one picture of how it might appear. Just as there is no universal definition of inclusion, neither is there universal agreement on what true inclusion looks like. There is no single, ideal model of inclusion. So do not go looking for one. When working with schools to provide inclusive opportunities for students with disabilities, however, there are some definite tenets that we follow.

What are the general principles of inclusion?

First, we believe that schools are communities and are a reflection of society. In our schools, approximately 10% of students have been identified as having disabilities that require special education services (Hallahan & Kauffman, 2000). We can extrapolate that figure to the general population and suggest that about 10% of people in our society have disabilities. General education classrooms should typically contain no more than this percentage of students with disabilities. If the number is much greater, the classroom does not reflect society and becomes more of a special education classroom in which individuals without disabilities have been included. Class sizes should be taken into consideration. We believe that for inclusion to be truly successful, class size should not exceed 20 students.

Second, students should attend the school that their brothers and sisters do, or the school that they would attend if they did not have a disability. Many students with disabilities are bussed to schools outside of their neighborhood, while their siblings or peers attend a different school or district. It becomes increasingly difficult for students to develop peer relationships with typical children who live within close proximity to them if they do not attend school with typical students. Additionally, if students with disabilities do not attend the same school with their peers, it is not likely that they will develop relationships outside of school with them.

Third, it has been our experience that in some schools where inclusive practices are not embraced and encouraged by all individuals, students with disabilities are thought of as different than the typical students. A "yours" and "ours" mentality seems to prevail in many, but not all, schools. Students with disabilities are thought to belong to special education staff and are referred to as "those" or "your" students by general education staff and administrators. In an inclusive school, where there is a true sense of community, *all* personnel are responsible for *all* students. Principals, classroom teachers, specialists, etc., all take responsibility for the education and discipline of all students with or without disabilities. All children are thought of and considered to be "our" students.

Finally, a teacher in an inclusive classroom utilizes *best* and *effective* teaching practices and, with *appropriate support, resources,* and *materials,* can teach all students, whether the students are gifted and talented, at-risk, typical, or have disabilities. Chapter 4 will discuss, in detail, effective teaching practices and appropriate support, resources, and materials necessary to make inclusion successful for all those involved.

Does inclusion work?

We, as educators, believe that inclusionary practices are effective for all students. There are many educators who believe that separate education or instruction for students with disabilities does not work and can even be harmful for *all* students. And conversely, many educators are concerned that including students with disabilities in the classroom will impact negatively on the learning of nondisabled students. A number of studies dispute these concerns.

Baker, Wang, & Walberg (1995) compared the effectiveness of general education class placements to special class placements from pre-1980 to the 1990s. Results showed that placement in general education settings had positive effects on the academic and social development of nondisabled students. In a study conducted by McDonnell, Thorson, McQuivey, & Kiefer-O'Donnell (1991), which evaluated the levels of academic engagement between elementary students with disabilities and their nondisabled peers, results indicated that students with disabilities become more meaningfully involved in the academic activities of the general education classroom when included. Their presence does not appear to impede the academic involvement of nondisabled students in the class.

Sharpe, York, & Knight (1994) found no differences in the performance of regular education students (K–6) educated in inclusive classrooms compared to those educated in noninclusive classrooms. Centre & Curry (1993) compared the effects of a special educator providing support to students with disabilities and low-achieving students in the regular education classroom in Grades 3–6 to a similar control group with no support. Results indicated slightly higher scores on posttests for the group receiving support and higher scores in social interaction. This research shows the importance of support for the classroom teacher.

Who benefits from inclusion?

The aforementioned research certainly suggests that the answer to this question is that *all* students benefit from inclusion. Research indicates that students with disabilities benefit academically as well as socially. It seems only natural that if a person feels a sense of belonging and acceptance, that person will be more likely to strive and grow.

Hehir (1995) found that programs that give special education teachers and paraprofessionals the opportunity to work in general education classrooms with students with and without disabilities resulted in an "incidental benefit" to typical students. The benefits included additional teacher support, opportunities to learn about human differences, and instructional adaptations.

In a review of the research on the effects of inclusion on nondisabled students, Peck & Staub (1994) found that there is no deceleration of academic progress for nondisabled children enrolled in inclusive classrooms. They report that many nondisabled students experienced a growth in their commitment to personal moral and ethical principles as a result of their relationships with students with disabilities. The research also showed that nondisabled students' fears of students with disabilities decreased, and comfort with and awareness of differences increased.

This research supports the assertion that students with and without disabilities benefit from being educated together in the general education classroom. Students with disabilities have an opportunity to be part of the school community and to learn from and with their nondisabled peers. Typical students learn to accept, understand, welcome, and work with students with disabilities. The development of all children is enhanced by the extent to which they feel a sense of belonging, caring, and community in school (Noddings, 1984). The students of today are our future leaders, taxpayers, service providers, and parents. The degree to which they learn about understanding and communicating with peers who have diverse backgrounds, abilities, and needs will impact the way in which they interact with others as adults (Brown et al., 1991).

Chapter 2 will examine further the perceptions of various constituencies (teachers, students, parents, and administrators) on inclusion, and how these perceptions have been shaped and changed over the years.

References

Baker, E. T., Wang, M. C., & Walberg, H. J. (1995). The effectives of inclusion on learning. *Educational Leadership, 52*(4), 33–35.

Brown, L., Schwarz, P., Udarvi-Solner, A., Kampschroer, E. F., Johnson, F., Jorgenson, J., & Gruenewald, L. (1991). How much time should students with severe intellectual disabilities spend in regular education classrooms and elsewhere? *Journal of the Association for Persons with Severe Handicaps, 16*(1), 39–47.

Brown v. Board of Education of Topeka, 347 U.S. 483, 74 Sup. Ct. 686. (1954).

Centre, Y., & Curry, C. (1993). A feasibility study of a full integration model developed for a group of students classified as mildly intellectually disabled. *International Journal of Disability, Development and Education, 40*(3), 217–235.

Hallahan, D., & Kauffman, J. (2000). *Exceptional learners: Introduction to special education.* Needham Heights, MA: Allyn & Bacon.

Hehir, T. (1995). *Improving the individual with disabilities education act: IDEA reauthorization (draft).* Washington, DC: Office of Special Education and Rehabilitative Services.

Individuals with Disabilities Education Act, 20 U.S.C. 1400 et seq. (1997). Washington, DC: U. S. Government Printing Office.

Lipsky, D. K., & Gartner, A. (1996). *Inclusive education and school restructuring.* In W. Stainback & S. Stainback (Eds.). *Controversial issues confronting special education: Divergent perspectives.* Needham Heights, MA: Allyn and Bacon.

Maslow, A. H. (1968). *Toward a psychology of being: The farther reaches of human nature.* New York: John Wiley & Sons.

McDonnell, T., Thorson, N., McQuivey, C., & Keifer-O'Donnell, R. (1997). Academic engaged time of students with low-incidence disabilities in the general education classroom. *Mental Retardation, 35*(1), 18–26.

Noddings, N. (1984). *Caring: A feminine approach to ethics and moral education.* Berkeley, CA: University of California Press.

Peck, C. A., & Staub, D. (1994). What are the outcomes for nondisabled students? *Educational Leadership, 52*(4), 36–40.

Rogers, J. (1993). The inclusion revolution. *Phi Delta Kappan Research Bulletin, 11*, 1–6.

Sharpe, M. N., York, J. L., & Knight, J. (1994). Effects of inclusion on the academic performance of classmates without disabilities. *Remedial and Special Education, 15*(5), 281–287.

Stainback, S., & Stainback, W. (1992). *Curriculum considerations in inclusive classrooms: Facilitating learning for all students.* Baltimore: Paul H. Brookes.

U.S. Department of Education. (2001). *Twenty-third annual report to Congress on the implementation of the individuals with disabilities education act.* Washington, DC.

Perspectives on Inclusion

If inclusion is the "right thing to do," why do people have so many concerns?

The move to an inclusive philosophy is a major paradigm shift. Educators are rethinking the way they view and evaluate education for students with disabilities. For many years, from the 19th through the first half of the 20th century, students with disabilities were educated in separate classrooms or facilities (Karagiannis, Stainback, & Stainback, 1996). It was believed that students with disabilities were better taught "with their own kind," and that they required special teaching approaches, curriculum, and materials. Hahn (1989) referred to the educational approach at that time as the "functional limitations" approach. The focus was on the students' deficits. The role of the educator was to try to fix students' problems. For these students, the future was limited. Students with learning disabilities were not expected to go to college. Students with significant cognitive deficits were not expected to ever function independently.

An inclusive philosophy is a shift in thinking about how and what students with disabilities can learn. It has, at its core, the belief that all students can learn in and can benefit from the general education classroom and curriculum. Components of this philosophy have been delineated in chapter 1. Changes in the way we think about the education of students with disabilities come with increased responsibility and accountability. If expectations for students are raised, educators, parents, and students must rise to the challenge. With increased expectations comes fear of failure, and it is because of this that many parents and professionals are resistant to an inclusive model because they believe that services can be delivered more appropriately in other settings. Parents fear failure for their children, and educators fear they will not be able to meet students' needs. With any major shift in service delivery comes the consideration of costs. Administrators and consumers ask if it will be more costly or more cost-effective to implement an inclusive model. A major question in everyone's mind is, Will this lead to a weaker, watered-down curriculum for all students?

This chapter will delineate in more detail the concerns of the various constituents about an inclusive model and philosophy. We will attempt to address those concerns and identify the key factors in addressing the worries of the constituents. Through an understanding of the fears of others, we will be better able to work together to meet the goals of all students.

Why should we think inclusively?

The social implications of inclusion mean that we should embrace each student in the school as an integral member of that school community. "The issue of integration [inclusion] is an important one. It provides an opportunity for raising serious questions about the kind of society we desire and the nature and functions of schooling…" (Barton & Landman, 1993, p. 41). Schools are microcosms of society, preparing students for a future in a community that does not separate the disabled from the nondisabled. It is important that students learn in school how to work and live together—the ultimate test for their future.

Who are the "stakeholders" in an inclusionary school?

Since inclusion involves the whole school and the community, stakeholders include students, parents, teachers, administrators, and taxpayers. All of these constituencies have a "stake" in the implementation and the successes and failures of an inclusive philosophy.

What does each group of constituents have to gain or lose from inclusion?

In order to answer this question, in the next section of this chapter we will consider the perspectives of each group of constituents. The benefits and the drawbacks of inclusion will be considered for each of the groups.

What are the students' perspectives on inclusions?

When answering this question, the perspectives of students with and without disabilities should be considered. Students with disabilities often feel ambivalent about being included in the general education classroom alongside their "typical" peers. On one hand, they enjoy the close proximity to all students in their age group and in their grade at school. The opportunity for developing relationships and friendships cannot exist if students are not interacting with each other in various settings. School is a social setting that consumes a great deal of a child's day.

On the other hand, learning alongside their peers can often highlight differences in students' learning. Students struggling with reading might worry about being asked to take their turn to read aloud or to share written work aloud. When implemented effectively, however, students with a wide range of needs and abilities will be embraced by their peers. When it is not implemented well, students can feel isolated and their self-esteem may suffer. Some students prefer to be in a separate class alongside other students with disabilities. They feel that their disability will be less of an issue in a segregated setting.

In this chapter, we will illustrate what inclusion looks like through the use of vignettes or case studies loosely based on students, parents, and teachers with whom we have worked. The first vignette illustrates the fact that inclusion is not a panacea. Inclusion does not magically solve all of the problems a student with a disability may encounter in school. It does demonstrate how inclusion can build understanding and support for a youngster with learning difficulties, rather than hiding the issues.

Mark may never totally escape being teased while in school. But if his teachers work to build acceptance and understanding of his disability, all of

---

Vignette 1: Feeling different

Mark is a 9-year-old boy who is an excellent baseball player and enjoys being with his friends at recess and after school. He has a significant reading disability and he has been included in a general education classroom each year. During reading and in all subjects where students are asked to read orally, Mark becomes very anxious that he might be called upon to read. The other students often tease him about his reading performance. Mark has a modified reading program and his classmates make fun of him for reading the "baby books." Mark is not the only student in his class who has difficulty with reading, but he sometimes says that he feels that he must be the "stupidest."

Mark's situation can be dealt with in two ways:

1. He could be removed from the regular classroom during reading time. This will enable him to complete reading assignments without the fear of being ridiculed. The disadvantage of pulling Mark out of the classroom is that he will probably still be embarrassed about leaving his class to go to the special education room—or "dummy" room, as his classmates refer to it. While he is out of the classroom, he misses out on teaching opportunities offered to his nondisabled peers. And while many educators may be reluctant to admit this, oftentimes a separate curriculum is less difficult and may not be challenging students with disabilities to reach their full potential.

2. Mark could remain in his general education classroom. Special education is a service—not a place. Specialized instruction can be delivered in the regular classroom. By exploring with the entire class their various strengths, abilities, and challenges, Mark's teacher can provide opportunities to highlight the areas in which Mark and other students excel. If and when other students taunt him, an open discussion can take place in the classroom about understanding the differences in the way we learn. Mark can, if he wishes, explain what he understands about his disability to his classmates.

the students will benefit, and they will hopefully be more tolerant of others with disabilities throughout their lives.

The notion of building support and acceptance through the proximity of students with disabilities to their nonhandicapped peers does not guarantee social success. This proximity may foster some negative behaviors that often grow out of a lack of understanding about disabilities. Students make fun of others often because they don't understand them, or because they are not feeling very confident about themselves. At the heart of an inclusive classroom is the building of understanding and acceptance of all students. Discussions should take place about how all individuals are different, and about how we all have certain strengths and limitations. This could be part of a social skills curriculum, or a unit on understanding differences and disabilities. But it is far more meaningful if these discussions take place as part of normally occurring events in the day. If a student is made to feel embarrassed or uncomfortable for any reason, then that is the time when a discussion on acceptance of differences should take place.

Lipsky & Gartner (1996) note that, as with other groups who have been disadvantaged over the years, individuals with disabilities are attempting to alter previously perceived negative characteristics into positive attributes. People with disabilities—and advocates of those with disabilities—are attempting to promote "disability" as just another aspect of the human condition. A disability is another difference in our society to be recognized, understood, and accepted—just as we understand and accept differences in ethnic backgrounds, languages, and race. Building this understanding—and our ability to work together—should be one of the primary goals of our schools.

Students without disabilities who have been involved in an inclusionary model from their first days in school see this model as a way of life. In a study done by Schnorr (1990) of a first-grade classroom where a youngster with severe disabilities was included, the students were, in general, unaffected by the students with significant special needs. Their response to his presence, as typified in the title of Schnorr's article "*Peter? He Comes and Goes...*" (Schnorr, 1990), illustrates how little the students feel affected by this youngster's presence. As students grow older—and as academic demands increase—students with significant behavioral issues may affect the performance of the "typical" student in the classroom. In such cases, it is imperative that a careful and extensive behavioral assessment and plan be developed. In situations where a student's behavior may disrupt other students' performance on a test or other high-stakes task, the potentially disruptive student should be assigned to an alternative task, possibly outside the classroom. Too often, however, teachers are quick to remove a student without fully understanding what is causing the disruptive behavior to occur. Such behavior could, for example, serve as an effective communication strategy for students who desire to leave the classroom when they feel high anxiety. In such cases, the undesirable behavior is being reinforced by removing the student from the area.

Students without disabilities have much to gain from being with their peers who have disabilities. It has already been mentioned that the "typical" student will gain a greater knowledge, understanding, and acceptance of differences in human beings. They will have the opportunity to learn how their peers cope with the challenges of disabilities, serving as role models in coping with adversity. The students without disabilities will also have an opportunity for the increased responsibility of supporting others as they serve as peer tutors and counselors (Rogers, 1993).

Some students without disabilities—particularly as they enter the high school years—raise concerns about the rigor of the curriculum when students with disabilities are included. Students without disabilities have the pressure of high-stakes testing, college entrance requirements, and preparation for college courses weighing heavily on their minds. If the curriculum is significantly altered or changed to meet the needs of students with disabilities, the question is raised as to whether or not the curriculum is challenging the more capable students. When inclusive practices are implemented appropriately, the curriculum remains the same, and adequate support is provided. All students in the classroom benefit from additional staff and resources. General education teachers and special education teachers come together to determine exciting and effective strategies to meet the needs of the entire class—for those with and without disabilities. Chapters 3, 4, and 5 of this text will illustrate how a flexible curriculum and teaching strategies can ensure that all students will gain what they need in an inclusive classroom.

How do parents feel about inclusion?

When their child with a disability reaches school age, professionals are likely to give parents very different opinions about the best placement for their youngster (Hobbs & Westling, 1998). Turnbull & Ruef (1997) asked parents their views on their experiences with teachers and administrators regarding inclusive educational approaches and their child. The results were very disheartening. Many parents reported that they felt pushed into placing their child into more restrictive environments. Parents completing this survey expressed overwhelming concern that the statutes of the law (IDEA) were not being fully implemented in support of their child's program.

While every parent may have the dream of a traditional education and success in school for their child, their expectations, upon understanding that their child has a disability, can be quite different. Their responses generally fall into two categories:

a) *Parents who want and expect their child to learn in the general education classroom*

Most parents expect that their child will attend the local elementary school with their neighborhood friends. They look forward to having their child make friends and learn from and with their friends. To hear that your child will have to go to a different school *because* of a disability can be a very discouraging and frustrating experience. Parents may react by insisting that their child attend the local school in which their child's peers are enrolled. In particular, parents who understand that the law requires that their child be educated in the least restrictive environment will exercise their child's rights and insist that he or she be placed in an inclusive setting with the supports needed to succeed. Parents who want their child in an inclusive setting may share the same dream as other parents for their child to graduate from high school, or even from college. They don't want their child to learn a different curriculum. They may fear that if their child is not challenged, he or she will never learn.

b) *Parents who worry that their child's needs may not be met unless he or she receives specialized services in a special classroom*

We have found that parents who lean toward a more restrictive placement do so because they feel that, at a minimum, they can be assured that their child will be getting specialized services. Green & Shinn (1995) report that some parents are concerned that placement in the general education classroom will result in a loss of individualized services usually received in the resource room. Parents also worry about their child being ridiculed and verbally abused by other students.

Parents who resist an inclusive educational model are often afraid that their child's needs are so unique and different that they will best be met in a special school or class with other children who have similar needs. They fear that placing their child in a classroom where the general education curriculum is being taught will result in their child falling even further behind when the curriculum does not meet their child's needs. They believe that a different curriculum and specialized materials are essential if their child's needs are to be met.

Some parents of nondisabled students feel that their child's education will be compromised if educated alongside students with disabilities. They feel the needs of the students with disabilities will disrupt their child's education and safety. They are concerned that the teacher will become too occupied in dealing with the students with disabilities and not attend to their child. However, teachers report that once these fears are allayed, parents typically become supporters of inclusion programs (Phillips, Sapona, & Lubic, 1995). Peck, Hayden, Wandschneider, Peterson, & Richarz (1990) found that parents familiar with inclusion indicate that nondisabled students benefit from their relationships with individuals with disabilities. This, too, has been our experience.

Vignette 2: Making the right decision

Alyssa Barrett has cerebral palsy, and when she began school Alyssa was placed in a special class where it was felt her needs would be best met. While the Barretts thought Alyssa could be better challenged, they deferred to the judgment of the experts when making a decision about Alyssa's placement.

When Alyssa turned eight years old, the Barretts moved to a new community. The Barretts were surprised when, in Alyssa's new school, an inclusive placement was suggested. After experiencing the services of a specialized segregated program, they were concerned that Alyssa's academic needs would not be met and that Alyssa would find it difficult to be accepted by the other children. After a few months, Mrs. Barrett called Alyssa's classroom teacher to report that Alyssa had been invited to her first birthday party. Mrs. Barrett was ecstatic! Her joy was buoyed even further when at the end of the year Alyssa had made significant progress in her reading skills. In her previous school, she had been given a very basic and limited reading program because it was assumed that Alyssa's skills would always be quite limited. Her exposure to a rich literature and language environment as well as various reading approaches with the other children, coupled with a modified curriculum and specific reading strategies to address her disability, have led to Alyssa's success.

When Alyssa was about to enter the sixth grade, Mrs. Barrett's work necessitated that the family make another move. This time the Barretts were certain of the model of schooling that they wanted for Alyssa. Unfortunately, they met with great resistance in their new school district. It has been an uphill battle to keep Alyssa involved in the general education classes. The Barretts' persistent advocacy for their daughter has led to an adversarial relationship with the school. It has been difficult for the Barretts to understand why personnel in this latest school do not share their optimism about Alyssa's potential.

As educators, we may not share the same perspective as a parent. We may fall into the trap of considering ourselves the experts on education and learning. The parents, however, are the "experts" in understanding their child. Whether we think the parents' expectations are too low, or unrealistically high, we must learn to accept the fact that the placement of the student is the parents' decision, and we must learn to best meet the needs of the student in whatever setting the child is in (Hobbs & Westling, 1998).

In order for any educational model to be effective, parents and educators must work together to achieve success. A study conducted by Epstein (1995) found that teachers and administrators want to have positive relationships with parents, but many are not confident about their ability to do so and they ultimately end up not trying. Epstein refers to a "rhetoric rut," noting that educators express support for partnerships but that they take no action in creating them. A concerted effort to build trust and mutual respect is necessary for the development of an educational environment that will support parents regardless of the educational model they select for their child.

How do teachers feel about inclusion?

Teachers' opinions on inclusion, just like those of parents, often fall on both sides of the inclusion issue. Teachers who support inclusion recognize the social and emotional benefits that students gain when they live, play, and learn alongside their "typical" peers. These teachers have likely had the preparation needed to make accommodations or modifications in their teaching that will support all students' learning. Over time, teachers who have been involved with inclusive education report a change in their attitude toward the learning abilities of students with disabilities. They are often surprised by the academic gains of their students with learning difficulties, reporting that these students' gains far exceeded their expectations (Snyder, Garriot, & Aylor, 2001).

Some teachers see inclusion as an opportunity to grow professionally and personally. It is an opportunity to collaborate in teaching, which can be both stimulating and enjoyable. Inclusion offers each teacher the opportunity to learn from one another. Historically, special education and general education teachers have participated in a system that divides and separates teachers in the same way it isolates and categorizes students.

An effective inclusion model requires that the full professional team—special education teachers, general education teachers, related service providers, support personnel, administrators, and parents—work together in delivering educational services. Teachers who do not support an inclusive educational model typically have had no experience or preparation in working with students with disabilities. They may feel self-doubt about their ability to be an effective member of an educational team and to meet the needs of students with disabilities. There may be territorial issues or a lack of trust between teachers who are accustomed to teaching alone in their classroom behind closed doors (Rainforth, York, & Macdonald, 1992; Wood, 1998). General education teachers may see inclusion as creating a "dumping ground" out of their classroom (Walther, Korinek, McLaughlin, & Williams, 2000). Students who would previously leave the class for specialized instruction, or who have significant behavioral and social issues, are now part of the classroom teacher's responsibility. With so many demands placed on teachers to prepare diverse students for high-stakes assessments, and to meet the expanding requirements of statewide initiatives, it is no wonder that many classroom teachers view inclusion as an added burden.

Vignette 3: When it works…

Angela, a high school teacher who has been teaching for 20 years, was reluctant to have her school move toward an inclusion model. Her new and energetic principal arrived with all kinds of ideas, one of which was to eliminate most special education classes. Special education teachers would move into the general education classroom to support students with disabilities. Angela had several questions and concerns about this model:

1. Would the students with special needs be able to keep up with her curriculum?

2. Would she have to "water down" the curriculum, thereby jeopardizing the performance of her other students in statewide testing?

3. Would she be able to meet the needs of these new students? After all, she had had no training in special education.

4. Would she be able to work with the special education teacher assigned to her? She was used to working on her own, doing her own thing in the confines of her own classroom. How would this work? Would it work?

Just about all of her misgivings were laid to rest after several years of working in an inclusive model. Before the change took place, all of the teachers attended workshops to help them understand the needs of students with disabilities. The teachers were given a wealth of information about how to modify and adapt their teaching methods. They learned strategies such as cooperative learning and teaching toward multiple intelligences that benefited *all of the students* in their classrooms. Angela was paired with a special education teacher, Marcia, who shared her view of high standards and her enjoyment of the students. She learned to appreciate the opportunity to brainstorm ideas with Marcia. What was most amazing was the progress that the students with disabilities made, and the pride they demonstrated in their ability to meet new challenges. There were times when Angela felt disheartened for the students with disabilities who just couldn't seem to grasp a concept, or who were teased by peers when they saw them struggling. But, over time, she saw an improvement in the relationships between students with and without disabilities. She used teasing episodes as opportunities for talking with students about building understanding and respect. She also saw the students appreciate each others' gifts as her creative teaching allowed students to demonstrate their knowledge in creative ways, fostered by a multiple intelligences approach. It was a lot of work for her, but the rewards were great as she felt better about her teaching and observed students' gains, both academically and socially. Angela had to admit that, in the end, it was worth it.

When it doesn't work...

Tim, a fourth-grade teacher who is new to this district that has embraced "total inclusion," supports this philosophy but is having a difficult time with the implementation. Due to budget cuts, he has 28 students in his class. Twelve of his students have IEPs. Two of them present significant behavioral challenges and one is diagnosed with attention deficit hyperactivity disorder (ADHD). He suspects that the other student with behavioral issues may also have ADHD, but the child's parents are refusing to pursue diagnosis. Tim was told he would have the support of a paraprofessional, but that position was eliminated with the budget cuts. He does have the support of a special education teacher a few hours each day, but she is often busy testing or attending meetings, and when she is around, she seems as overwhelmed as he is. Tim and his colleagues have virtually no time to plan together, and professional development opportunities are minimal. Most disheartening is the fact that all of Tim's students are struggling and becoming discouraged. Tim is thinking that he may not return to this district next year—and perhaps not to teaching at all!

From the scenarios presented above, it is clear that for an inclusion model to succeed, teachers must have the support and training needed to be effective in meeting the needs of a diverse group of students. Otherwise, they fear they will not be successful. That fear can be demonstrated through resistance or anger toward any efforts to include students with disabilities. With the right support, teachers will embrace an inclusive philosophy because it leads to success (Scruggs & Mastropieri, 1996). In a 1995 survey asking teachers about future directions in the education of students with disabilities, there was significant agreement among the participants that inclusion will continue and that schools will become more inclusive in the future (Putnam, Spiegel, & Bruininks, 1995). "Change is a process that requires teachers to reach new understandings about their work, its purpose, how to accomplish it, and how their work connects with others…" (Janney, Snell, Beers, & Raynes, 1995, p. 437).

How do administrators feel about inclusion?

Administrators' views on inclusion often fall along the same lines as teachers' views. They may have had little exposure to inclusion and do not understand why and how students with disabilities can succeed in the general education classroom. Their training both as a teacher and as an administrator may not have addressed inclusionary practices. Superintendents often consider the resources needed to support students with disabilities as a drain on their budget. Principals see themselves in a "we vs. they" situation, where they are caught in the middle between staff and parents who support inclusion and those who do not. Add to this the multiple pressures administrators face to increase students' test scores, and the notion of having more students with disabilities in the general education classroom is not very popular.

We have found, and our experience is supported in the literature (Shaffner & Busewell, 1996), that administrators play a major role in the successful implementation of an inclusive model. A principal with a positive attitude who models a "How can we do it?" attitude, rather than asking "Why do we have to do it?" will be better able to lead his or her staff to the appropriate problem-solving processes to make inclusion work. The principal can help teachers identify the resources they have in the school and consider how they can most effectively be used to implement an inclusive philosophy. Budget constraints, a lack of staff, and negative attitudes can all serve as challenges to promoting inclusion, but they can be surmounted when everyone—with the principal leading the initiative—embraces inclusion as essential for all students.

Vignette #4 illustrates the ways in which an inclusive philosophy can create a positive environment for the entire school. The community spirit and positive approach will help all students to feel welcome. Administrators who create a separatist environment will find the creation of a community spirit among their staff to be a major challenge.

Vignette 4: Portrait of an inclusive school

The Lincoln School is viewed as a school in a large urban district that fully supports inclusion. Everyone embraces this philosophy, but it begins with the special education director, Ms. Allen, and the principal, Mr. Joyce. These two individuals have worked together to pool their resources to creatively meet the needs of all learners in the school. Teachers who apply for a position at the school are informed that they will be expected to embrace and implement an inclusionary model. When problems arise with any student, with or without disabilities, the principal is actively involved with staff in finding a resolution. Anyone who enters this school is struck by the sense of community and true joy in the celebration of differences and the mutual respect among students and staff.

How do taxpayers feel about inclusion?

When the movement to inclusion began a few decades ago, some community members saw it as a cost-saving move. They would be able to place more students with disabilities in the general education classroom and thus reduce the need for special education teachers. This, however, has not necessarily been the case. In fact, an inclusive model can, initially, be more costly than other service delivery models. Instead of having a group of students meet with the special education teacher at one time in a separate classroom, the special education teacher is expected to provide support to students when they are in various classrooms throughout the building. This model initially requires additional special education support, either through the use of paraprofessionals or additional special education teachers. Lipsky & Gartner (1996) suggest that, over time, an inclusive model can be more effective, and more cost-effective. In the long run, however, the net gain of having students who are challenged alongside their typical peers—and who can work together—far outweighs the financial costs of inclusion. In the long run, students who are held to tougher standards—rather than different, perhaps lower standards—will be more productive members of the community and less of a drain on taxpayers' resources.

Some schools have faced the cost challenge by creating innovative scheduling that allows special educators maximum opportunities to support students in a variety of settings. For example, since special education support is most needed during reading instruction, ensuring that reading instruction is not taught at the same time in every classroom allows the special education teacher more opportunities to provide support where it is needed.

Our society has created an educational system that for many years was built upon a philosophy of exclusion. For many years, students of different race were expected to attend different public schools. Similarly, special schools have been created to meet every type of disability. Most educators today experienced or witnessed some of those exclusionary policies in their days as students. It is difficult to change a system that has so permeated our lives and our way of thinking. Just as we cannot imagine separate classes for students of Caucasian, Asian, or African-American descent, we should not consider such an arrangement for students just because they have a disability. The following sections of this chapter will address the rationale for the inclusive model.

Given the different perspectives of the stakeholders, what are the key factors that move us toward inclusionary practices in schools?

A summary of the positions of various stakeholders, both favorable and unfavorable to inclusion, can be found in Figure 2.1.

Figure 2.1

Stakeholders' perspectives on inclusion

Stakeholder Group	*Potential* Gains/Positives	*Potential* Losses/Concerns
Students— "Typical"	• Broader social and academic experiences • Additional professional and support personnel in classes • Greater range of teaching, approaches, and materials	• Loss of instructional time due to disruptions or instructional needs of students with disabilities • Lowering of academic standards
Students with Disabilities	• Academic and social role models • Greater opportunities for social interactions in and out of school • Access to the general education curriculum • Higher academic standards	• Loss of individualized instruction • Decreased access to specialized materials and services • Less opportunity to socialize with other students with disabilities • Struggles with academic learning more obvious to typical peers

Figure 2.1

Stakeholders' perspectives on inclusion *(Continued)*

Stakeholder Group	*Potential* Gains/Positives	*Potential* Losses/Concerns
Parents	• Potential for children to meet/make friends • Appropriate role models for language development and behavior • Curriculum is more challenging	• Concern that special services will not be adequately provided • Child will be teased and ridiculed for their disability • Curriculum will be too demanding
Teachers	• Benefits to all students, academically and socially • Additional support and team teaching model improve instruction for all	• Feel they are not prepared to meet the challenge • Not provided adequate support • Stronger students will fall behind • Students with disabilities will not have their needs met
Administrators	• Creative teaching environment leads to success for all • Atmosphere of community benefits all • Creative use of resources allows more students to benefit	• Insufficient resources will lead to failure • Administrators and teachers are not prepared to meet the challenge
Taxpayers	• Not necessarily more costly • Long-term benefits of challenging curriculum and development of positive attitudes outweigh minuses and costs, if any	• Concern over costs • Concern that typical students will not be held to a high enough standard

As can be clearly seen in Figure 2.1, not all of the stakeholders agree on whether we should be practicing an inclusionary philosophy. Whether or not agreement exists, inclusion must continue as part of the basic philosophy in our schools because: a) we all need to feel membership in our community, b) inclusion mirrors our way of life, c) it reflects the future of our society, and d) it has its basis in the law. Each of these points will now be addressed.

a) *The need for membership*

We all share a need for membership in our lives. Whether at work, in our family, or in school, we all feel a need to belong to the group with which we are involved. Students with disabilities often feel membership in every community in which they are involved—except for school. It is at school that their differences in learning become the negative focus in their lives. They are treated differently and they feel different. This image of themselves erodes their self-esteem, resulting in reduced motivation and interest in school (Stainback & Stainback, 1996). The long-term effects of being turned off to school are obvious. These students will graduate without the preparation needed to be successful members of the community. Since success in school is such an important measure of success in our society, these students may also go through life with an inferior view of themselves that could remain with them through adulthood.

Vignette 5: Feeling apart

Mike, a fourth grader, was delayed in learning how to read. His reading skills now seem to be at grade level, but he has difficulty in vocabulary development demonstrated by problems in oral and written communication. The curriculum of the fourth grade seems to be too much for him, and he was referred for testing. He was diagnosed with a language-based learning disability and problems with auditory processing. At his IEP meeting, it was decided that he should receive support from the speech pathologist to address his language problems. He was also referred to the special education resource room for support with the heavy reading demands and vocabulary expectations in his science and social studies classes.

One day the teacher called Mike's mother, Mrs. S., to tell her that Mike was refusing to leave the room for special services. Mrs. S. talked with him about this. Mike broke down saying, "I don't want to go to that room. The kids call it the 'dummy' room." When Mrs. S. reported this conversation to Mike's guidance counselor, she was told, "Oh no, Mrs. S., we don't have any of that teasing here." Obviously, Mike felt that they did.

Mike's story illustrates his need to feel the same as his peers. It also shows us that educators are not always in tune with students' or parents' concerns. If Mike's need for membership had been heard, strategies for making Mike feel a part of his school community could be discussed and his concerns could be addressed. Certainly, one step in meeting his needs would be to allow him to remain in his classroom—but not at the expense of his educational needs. Services could be provided to him within the context of his general educational classroom.

b) *Inclusion is a way of life*

When at work, we are not separated according to our IQ or our learning differences. We don't attend restaurants or movies according to our ability to read the menu or follow the plot. It is only in school where individuals are made to feel that their ability to learn is the most important aspect of their lives. Many students with disabilities may never go on to college, but they will work in the community. As they learn how to cope with their differences, and as we learn how to deal with the fact that we are all different, tolerance in school will grow with us into our adult life.

c) *The future of our society*

If we believe that the mission of schools is to develop the total person, then one of our major goals should be to build the type of character in students that will support tolerance and understanding of others. To that end, inclusion should not just be about accepting differences in how we learn, but in every aspect of our lives. It may be unrealistic for us to expect a totally harmonious society, but if we do not have that as our goal, then the ills of our current society will grow unchecked.

d) *A basis in the law*

There are many educators who feel that "inclusion" is just another trend or passing fad in education. There is a major difference between inclusion as a philosophical basis for education and other trends that have been based on unresearched philosophy. Inclusion is, as noted in chapter 1, the law. Based upon the findings of the Supreme Court in their decision of Brown v. the Board of Education of Topeka, Kansas (1954, 9.493), separate is not equal. When we place students in separate, more restrictive environments, we are not meeting the requirements of our legal system.

Inclusion is a means of building capacity within the system to better meet the needs of all learners. As we will see in chapters 3 and 4, inclusive classrooms are not successful unless they incorporate effective teaching approaches that meet a variety of learning styles and needs. Teachers who employ a variety of methodologies, who adapt curriculum when necessary and who are attentive to differences in learning, will be more successful with all students—not just those with disabilities. As one reviews the strategies noted in chapter 4, it will become evident that these are not "special strategies" reserved for students with disabilities. They are a list of proven and effective pedagogies that benefit all students.

References

Barton, L., & Landman, M. (1993). The politics of integration: Observations on the Warnock Report. In R. Slee (Ed.). *Is there a desk with my name on it? The politics of integration* (pp. 41–49). London: The Falmer Press.

Brown v. Board of Education of Topeka, 347 U.S. 483, 74 Sup. Ct. 686. (1954).

Epstein, J. L. (1995). School/family/community partnerships: Caring for the children we share. *Phi Delta Kappan, 76*(9), 701–717.

Green, S. K., & Shinn, M. R. (1994). Parent attitudes about special education and reintegration: What is the role of student outcomes? *Exceptional Children, 61*(3), 269–281.

Hahn, H. (1989). *The politics of special education.* In D. Lipsky & A. Gartner (Eds.). *Beyond Special Education* (pp. 225–242). Baltimore: Paul H. Brookes.

Hobbs, T., & Westling, D. (1998). Promoting successful inclusion. *Teaching Exceptional Children, 31*(1), 46–51.

Individuals with Disabilities Education Act, 20 U.S.C. 1400 et seq. (1997). Washington, DC: U. S. Government Printing Office.

Janney, R. E., Snell, M. E., Beers, M. K., & Raynes, M. (1995). Integrating students with moderate and severe disabilities into general education classes. *Exceptional Children, 61,* 425–439.

Karagiannis, A., Stainback, W., & Stainback, S. (1996). *Rationale for inclusive schooling.* Baltimore: Paul H. Brookes.

Lipsky, D. K., & Gartner, A. (1996). *Inclusive education and school restructuring.* In W. Stainback & S. Stainback (Eds.). *Controversial issues confronting special education: Divergent perspectives.* Needham Heights, MA: Allyn and Bacon.

Peck, C. A., Hayden, L., Wandschneider, M., Peterson, K., & Richarz, S. (1989). Development of integrated preschools: A qualitative inquiry into sources of resistance among parents, administrators, and teachers. *Journal of Early Intervention, 13,* 353–364.

Phillips, L., Sapona, R. H., & Lubic, B. L. (1995). Developing partnerships in inclusive education: One school's approach. *Intervention in School and Clinic, 30,* 262–272.

Putnam, J., Spiegel, A., and Bruininks, R. (1995). Future directions in education and inclusion of students with disabilities: A Delphi investigation. *Exceptional Children, 61*(6), 553–576.

Rainforth, B., York, J., & Macdonald, C. (1992). *Collaborative teams for students with severe disabilities: Integrating therapy and educational services.* Baltimore: Paul H. Brookes.

Rogers, J. (1993). The inclusion revolution. *Phi Delta Kappan Research Bulletin, 11,* 1–6.

Scruggs, T. E., & Mastropieri, M. A. (1996). Teacher perceptions of mainstreaming/inclusion, 1958–1995: A research synthesis. *Exceptional Children, 63*(1), 59–74.

Shaffner, B., & Busewell, B. (1996). Ten critical elements for creating inclusive and effective school communities. In W. Stainback & S. Stainback (Eds.). *Inclusion: A guide for educators.* Baltimore: Paul H. Brookes.

Schnorr, R. F. (1990). "Peter? He comes and goes...": First graders' perspectives on a part-time mainstream student. *Journal of the Association for Persons with Severe Handicaps, 15*(4), 231–240.

Snyder, L., Garriot, P., & Aylor, M. W. (2001). Inclusion confusion: Putting the pieces together. *Teacher Education and Special Education, 24*(3), 198–207.

Turnbull, A., & Ruef, M. (1997). Family perspectives on inclusive life issues for people with problem behavior. *Exceptional Children, 63*(2), 211–217.

Walther, T. C., Korinek, L., McLaughlin, V., & Williams, B. (2000). *Collaboration for inclusive education.* Needham Heights, MA: Allyn and Bacon.

Wood, M. (1998). Whose job is it anyway? Educational roles in inclusion. *Exceptional Children, 64*(2), 181–195.

General Principles and Practices for Inclusion

Rethinking Curriculum

What is different about the curriculum for students with disabilities?

Federal law PL 105-17, The Individuals with Disabilities Education Act (IDEA), mandates that students with disabilities must have access to the same general education curriculum taught to all students, as well as to any education reform efforts that occur at the state, district, and local level. This means that all students—regardless of their disability—should be taught the curriculum that is defined for other students in the school district or state.

Previously, students with disabilities were not expected to meet the demands of the general education curriculum and were offered a different and less rigorous curriculum. Reasons for the differences in curriculum for students with and without disabilities were frequently based upon two assumptions:

1. The fact that some students *learn differently* caused some professionals to assume that these students couldn't learn *as much*, particularly in the case of students with severe disabilities.

2. Some professionals often automatically assumed that the general education curriculum would not be relevant for students with disabilities. They determined that a different curriculum would be more beneficial for students with disabilities. This separate curriculum, limited to functional skills, was deemed essential for students, such as preparing meals and counting change.

Separate classes for students with disabilities often adhered to a curriculum based upon these assumptions. With lowered expectations came lowered results. This chapter will attempt to illustrate that there is little need to have substantially different curricula for students with and without disabilities. As noted in chapters 1 and 2, students with disabilities have been very successful in general education classes with the general education curriculum. In fact, it has been mandated by federal law that all students must be prepared to learn the same curriculum and at the same level of standards. Chapter 4 will examine teaching strategies that help *all* students succeed with the general education curriculum, and chapter 5 illustrates the value of the Individualized Educational Program (IEP) in ensuring that all team members know what is needed to help a student with a disability to succeed.

It should be noted that the fact that students with disabilities are now mandated to receive the general education curriculum does not mean that they are limited to that curriculum. The development of functional skills should not be ignored. For students who need it, a combination of functional and general education curriculum should be provided. The integration of these approaches will be discussed later in this chapter.

How do we develop curriculum to meet the needs of all learners?

An effective curriculum is one that considers three data sources: the *learner's needs*, the *curriculum content* to be taught, and the *expectations of the society* in which the student lives (Tyler, 1969). Figure 3.1 illustrates how these three sources link together to create a student's goals. All three sources are important to the development of meaningful learner goals.

Figure 3.1   Illustration of Tyler's process in developing goals.

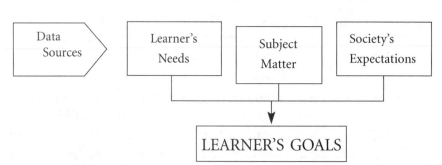

If any of the three sources are absent in the curriculum development process, the curriculum will be ineffective in preparing students for the future. The first data source, the learner, must be at the heart of the curriculum development process. If the learner's needs are not central to the curriculum development process, the curriculum will likely be irrelevant for the learner and will neither be understood nor learned.

The second data source that Tyler considers is the subject matter. Those who are knowledgeable in the subject matter must be part of the curriculum development process. In most states, subject matter specialists have developed curriculum guidelines for school districts to follow. These must drive the education of all students, regardless of their disability.

The expectations of society are another critical data source in the curriculum development process. Successful schools prepare students to be contributing members of society. If we do not consider what society's expectations are, we run the risk of having students graduate unprepared to meet the demands of their future. Recent education reform efforts have been driven, in large measure, by members of the business community who are committed to ensuring that graduates are well educated and ready for employment.

One outcome of this initiative by businesses has been the establishment of state standards that identify subject matter which must be learned and to serve as benchmarks for students' success (Garcia & Rothman, 2002). State standards establish a clearly delineated "bar" that students must meet to qualify for a high school diploma. These clearly defined expectations have had a major impact on what is taught and how it is taught to all students in schools.

The three data sources of Tyler's curriculum development model in Figure 3.1 were not originally developed with students with disabilities in mind, but they have great implications for an inclusionary school. An inclusionary school keeps the needs of all learners in mind while it prepares students for all aspects of the curriculum taught in schools. In preparing students for the expectations of today's society, an inclusionary school ensures that students are able to work in a very diverse society. In doing so, an inclusionary school promotes acceptance and understanding of all students. Tyler reminds us that the subject matter is also an important source in defining what is important to teach in schools. If students are not placed in settings that will help them gain access to the general education curriculum, we run the risk of not providing a viable curriculum. Even though Tyler's model was developed over 50 years ago with the general education population in mind, the three data sources serve as criteria for us to consider when ensuring the curriculum we develop is meaningful for all students.

In what environments should the curriculum be taught?

If students with disabilities are to be as successful as their nondisabled peers in learning the curriculum designed for all students, then a large part of their educational program must include full participation in the environments where other children are interacting and learning the general education curriculum. Therefore, the general education classroom is typically the most appropriate environment in which all students should learn. It is in the general education classroom where students can have full access to the general education curriculum. It is here that students with and without disabilities will learn from each other about appropriate communication and social skills. Students can learn academic skills together, although at times their individual objectives may be different.

As students grow older, they may demonstrate difficulty in meeting the demands of the general education curriculum. There may be times when students require specialized instruction that cannot be met in the regular classroom. Placement in a special education "resource room" may be required for part of the day to deliver highly specialized instruction. This may include instruction with specialized equipment or material. We caution, however, that removal from the general education classroom not be done until all avenues to provide instruction in the classroom have been attempted. Consider, for example, a student who is removed because they need a specialized reading approach. The reason for removal might be because the materials are not available in the classroom, or that it might be upsetting for the student to receive this instruction in the general education classroom, thereby highlighting a student's disability. Either of these reasons may be valid, but before removing the student, the educational team should consider: a) how the materials could be made available in the regular classroom, and b) how the other students in the classroom can be helped to understand the disability of the student in question, thereby building an understanding of differences.

As they grow older, students may also require more time in settings outside of school, such as work and community settings. As noted in the Tyler model (Figure 3.1), we need to look to the demands of society in preparing our students. For students with disabilities, this means that, as they grow older, they should be taught in settings that reflect the community in which they will live as adults. Figure 3.2 illustrates how, as students with severe disabilities grow older, more and more of their time is spent outside of the general education classroom.

Age 21

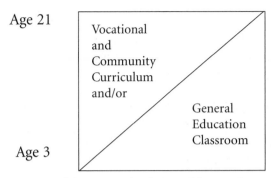

Figure 3.2 Illustration of relationship between age and educational setting for students with severe cognitive disabilities.

Age 3

Portion of time spent in class and in nonclassroom settings.

Students enrolled in special education qualify for services at age 3, and they remain eligible until age 21 (according to federal guidelines). At age 3, they should be included with their peers without disabilities 100% of the time. With young children, appropriate role models are essential. As they grow older, students with significant cognitive disabilities may require the integration of a more functional curriculum in their day, which *may* necessitate that some of their skills be learned outside of the general education classroom. For example, in elementary schools, a small part of a student's day may be spent on jobs in the school building outside of their classroom. In middle school, more time may be spent on jobs in the building. As they enter high school, jobs may be learned in the community. At age 18, when most of their peers leave high school for college, the students with severe cognitive disabilities spend all of their day outside of school learning skills at work and in the community under the supervision of job coaches and special education support personnel. The Individuals with Disabilities Education Act (IDEA, 1997) specifies aspects of IEP planning that will assist an educational team to prepare students for transition to the world of work. The regulations specify:

a) *transition services* means a coordinated set of activities for a student with a disability that:

1. Is designed within an outcome-oriented process, which promotes movement from school to postschool activities, including postsecondary education, vocational training, integrated employment (including supported employment), continuing and adult education, adult services, independent living, or community participation;

2. Is based on the individual student's needs, taking into account the student's preferences and interests; and

3. Includes (i) instruction, (ii) related services, (iii) community experiences, (iv) the development of employment and other postschool adult living objectives, and (v) if appropriate, acquisition of daily living skills and functional vocational evaluation.

b) Transition services for students with disabilities may be special education, if provided as specially designed instruction, or related services, if required to assist a student with a disability to benefit from special education. (IDEA, Subpart A, General, §300.29.)

The IDEA regulations make it very clear that the responsibility of the school goes beyond that of traditional academic planning and instruction. For older students with disabilities, the school must look beyond the classroom to the world of work. The "inclusionary environment" is extended to the community, including job locations. Educational preparation begins in the school, but gradually moves to the larger community in which the student lives. The student's role is integral to this process. A student's needs, interests, and abilities must be considered when preparing a student for the future.

Although not specified in the IDEA regulations, there are other transitions experienced by students with disabilities that should be considered and for which careful planning must take place. Moving to a new job, a new home, and community can be a challenge for any of us. For students with disabilities, such changes can be overwhelming. Students with disabilities who receive education in different environments every day must adjust to different teaching styles, different expectations, different terminology (particularly challenging for the many students who have a language-based disorder), etc. Minimizing the transitions students experience is yet another argument for inclusion. When transitions must occur, however, careful planning will assist the student with a disability to adjust and make the transition with greater ease. Schedules on the wall, with frequent references during the day to "what's next," can help a student psychologically prepare to move. Providing cues, such as "Five more minutes until we go to____," will give a student fair warning to prepare whatever materials need to be obtained and/or put away. Providing lists of what is needed to go from class to class will help students with organizational or memory problems. Taking the time to think about what challenges students face and helping them plan and prepare accordingly for changes in the day will go a long way toward helping them be successful in all environments.

When might a student receive services outside the general education classroom?

For the most part, particularly in the early grades, students should be educated in the general education classroom. Students with significant disabilities, as noted in Figure 3.2, may be removed from the classroom for part of the day to meet goals that are more vocationally or community oriented. We have also discussed in this chapter the occasional need for specialized instruction that *may* result in placement in a special education classroom or resource room.

There are other situations that may arise which would necessitate a student's being removed from a classroom. If their behavior is dangerous to themselves or others, they may need to be temporarily removed from the general education classroom. Or, if a student needs intrusive treatment that may impact on his or her dignity or need for privacy, such as nursing services, this may also be delivered outside the general education classroom. It is difficult to generate many examples of situations when a student's goals or objectives cannot be met in the general education classroom. Even when a student is not included in the general education classroom, however, the general education goals that are written for all students must be addressed. Federal guidelines for IEPs require that, if a student is to be educated outside of the general education classroom, an explanation must be provided in writing.

How do we design instruction to meet individual needs in the general education classroom?

It is challenging enough to think about how the classroom teacher can meet the needs of a diverse group of learners who do not have disabilities. Adding students with disabilities to the challenge can seem overwhelming. Specific changes in methodology may be necessary for students with disabilities to succeed in the general education classroom. Effective methods that are used with students with disabilities, such as a multisensory approach that supplements auditory instruction with visual cues, is effective teaching for all students. Not all students will require special methodology in all subject areas, and not all students will require specially designed instruction. Examples of effective teaching methods for inclusive classrooms will be described in more detail in chapter 4.

One tool to assist teachers in designing instruction for students with disabilities is the Individualized Educational Program (IEP). The IEP is mandated by

IDEA for students. A student's IEP must include ways in which the IEP goals and objectives link with the general education curriculum. If a student's goals do not connect with the general education curriculum, or if a student is to receive services outside the general education curriculum, a rationale must be provided. One of the key components of the IEP that will prove helpful to the classroom teacher is a description of the accommodations and/or modifications a student will need to meet his or her goals and objectives.[1]

What are accommodations and how are they determined for each student?

Students with mild or moderate disabilities, such as a learning disability, may be able to learn the same general curriculum as the rest of the class. For these students, *accommodations* may be necessary for them to learn the general education curriculum. Accommodations are changes in the delivery or implementation of the curriculum. With an accommodation, the student completes the assignment at the *same level* and with the *same expectations* as for the other students. The tools or processes teachers or students use may be different, but the content and learning goals remain the same. They may change how the students access or demonstrate learning, but they do not significantly alter the content of the curriculum and the concepts to be learned (Paulson & Fognani-Smaus, 1997). An example of an accommodation would be when a student with fine motor problems uses a computer to complete a writing assignment rather than a pen or pencil. Some students who have a reading disability may need more time to complete a test.

Many students are able to participate in the same curricular goals as their peers but will need different materials. This may vary from a pencil that is larger than those of other students, to the use of a computer for writing or a Braille typewriter. A student with a significant reading disability may, in content subjects, listen to a text on tape and be assessed through an oral, rather than a written, exam. The use of different materials does not mean that the student cannot learn the same concepts as those learned by fellow students.

What are curriculum modifications and how are they determined for each student?

Students with more significant disabilities will need substantial *modifications* to the learning and assessment process in the general education classroom.

---

[1] For more on the components of the IEP and the IEP process, see chapter 5.

A modification is a change in what a student is expected to learn and demonstrate (Paulson & Fognani-Smaus, 1997). A modification to the curriculum may actually alter the expectation of the student's performance. Paulson & Fognani-Smaus (1997) note that there are many forms of modifications. Students needing modifications may be working toward the same curriculum benchmark as their peers, but they may only meet a percentage of the key concepts of the benchmark. A modification might also mean that the student meets a standard at a different benchmark level, or a student might meet the standard through a parallel curriculum. For example, when students without disabilities are writing an essay to communicate their analysis of a reading selection, some students with significant disabilities may be writing a few words or pointing to pictures to illustrate the main ideas of a reading passage. Illustrations of the levels of three types of modifications are provided in Figure 3.3.

Figure 3.3 provides some examples of how a curriculum standard can be modified for a student who cannot meet that standard as written. The "Type of modification" column illustrates a progression of modification, with Level 1 being the more minimal modification and Level 3 illustrating the more significant modification to the standard as written. The examples show what these modifications might look like for a student. It is imperative that teachers utilize accommodations or modifications only when the students cannot participate in the curriculum in the same manner as their nondisabled peers. Accommodating must be the first consideration, followed by modifying, and only then if the student cannot benefit from participation in general education curriculum might an alternative activity be planned.

So the answer to the question, "What's different about the curriculum for students with disabilities?" is, "Very little!" All students should be working to achieve the standards delineated in the general education curriculum. For some students, alterations may be made, but *the essence* of the curriculum remains the same. The next section of this chapter will illustrate some ways in which we can rethink the process of curriculum development to include all learners and meet everyone's needs, regardless of individual strengths, challenges, or disabilities.

Figure 3.3 Modifications in what the student is expected to learn.

Illustration of Modification Types		
English language arts standard: *Students will demonstrate understanding of the dynamics, nature, structure, and history of the English language* **Benchmark:** *Students will pose questions, listen to the ideas of others, and contribute their own ideas in group discussions and interviews in order to acquire knowledge*		
What the class is doing	**Type of modification**	**Example of modification for a student with a disability**
Generating 10 questions on selected literature	Level 1: Meet standard at a lower performance level	Student formulates 6 research questions on a different, related—but more general—topic
Listening and responding to each others' answers to questions in a cooperative group	Level 2: Meet standard at different benchmark level	Answer multiple choice questions on a different, more general topic
Listening and responding to each others' questions in a cooperative group	Level 3: Meet intent of standard through access skills to the curriculum	Answer yes/no questions on likes/dislikes of a different and shorter passage

How do we ensure the learner's needs are met?

As noted by Tyler (1969), and discussed in an earlier section of this chapter, the learner's needs are most critical to effective curriculum development. This statement should appear to be obvious, but too often the academic needs of students with disabilities are overlooked when these students are included in the general education classroom.

Some students with significant disabilities are in general education classrooms for the purpose of "exposure" to their nondisabled peers. Little attention may be given to their academic needs. While proximity to typical students can certainly promote students' social and communication development, consideration must also be given as to how access to the general education curriculum can benefit students' learning needs in all aspects of development. We must ensure that all students' academic needs are being met, along with their social needs.

Stainback & Stainback (1992) suggest that this means rethinking the way we implement curriculum. So while curriculum standards are developed for all students, the way in which we address the standards must be linked to the learner's needs, abilities, and interests. This means that learning objectives must be flexible, and activities may need to be adapted.

One tool that we have found helpful to ensure that a student's individual goals will be met is the "activity/skills matrix." Many references have been made in the literature to the use of this simple tool, which clearly illustrates the relationship of a student's individual goals to his or her daily schedule of activities (Halvorsen & Neary, 2001). The activity matrix illustrates the various learning goals and objectives for a student, and indicates where, across the student's school day, these objectives can be taught.

Figure 3.4 exemplifies how the activity matrix has been used for Grace. Grace is a 14-year-old student in a comprehensive high school. She has been diagnosed as having autism. Some of Grace's goals and objectives are quite different from other students in the classes in which she is enrolled, but they can still be met in the same environments, as the activity matrix illustrates. For example, many of Grace's objectives reflect her oral and written communication needs. If the professional staff are made aware of these objectives, they can be mindful of them and address them in daily instruction. When she is in her algebra class, or world civilization, her academic goals may differ from those of other students, but she can still address the communication goals outlined in her IEP.

As you can see from the matrix, many opportunities exist across the day, which allow teachers to address Grace's goals. Even though Grace's objectives are quite different from the other students, she can still address her goals in the context of general education activities. Her social and communication objectives are addressed throughout the day in the context of classrooms where she is learning with her "typical" peers. Her peers serve as role models for her communication and social development. Peers may even become tutors or provide support as part of their participation in learning activities. For example, when working in cooperative groups, peers can ask Grace to summarize what was said, addressing Objective 8 in the activity matrix (Figure 3.4).

The activity/skills matrix can also be used as a checklist/monitoring sheet to indicate when each objective has been taught. As Grace progresses through her schedule of the day, the general education teacher, special education teacher, or paraprofessional can place a (x) on the block for each objective and where it was addressed. Data can also be entered into the block. For example, if Grace completes four sentences in English, the number 4 is entered

Figure 3.4 Activity matrix illustrating where Grace's goals/objectives can be taught across the day in a secondary school setting.

Activity/Skills Matrix for Grace

Subject/Activity	Objective 1 Write complete sentences	Objective 2 Calculate cost of up to 5 items with calculator	Objective 3 Add two-digit numbers	Objective 4 Attend to jobs/tasks for 20 min without requesting help	Objective 5 Copy personal data on job application	Objective 6 Respond to greetings/questions from others	Objective 7 Communicate with others making eye contact	Objective 8 Verbally summarize an experience using complete sentences
English	X			X	X	X	X	X
Algebra		X	X	X		X	X	X
World Civilization	X			X		X	X	X
Vocational Skills	X	X	X	X	X	X	X	X
Art				X		X	X	X
Environmental Science	X	X		X		X	X	X
Phys. Ed.				X		X	X	X

in the English block to record her responses. This information allows the teacher to see if Grace is making progress on her goals from day to day or week to week. This information becomes important for Grace's IEP team to make decisions for Grace's goals and objectives. Many of Grace's goals cannot be measured by paper and pencil tests. The information gathered on the activity/skills matrix can also be included in Grace's portfolio as part of an alternate means of assessing her progress.

The activity/skills matrix can also serve as a self-monitoring device for Grace. She can record data that reflects her performance and use it as a tool for self-evaluation. She can then reflect on her work and determine areas in which she needs to improve, identifying additional supports she might need.

Ensuring that Grace's individualized goals are met across the day is only one part of an effective curriculum development process. We also must ensure that Grace has access to the curriculum in all of her classes, even in challenging classes such as world civilization or algebra.

Sometimes a curriculum adaptation may be as simple as moving a child's position in the classroom or redesigning/rearranging the classroom to provide more options to meet the needs of more students. A student with visual or auditory problems will be more successful when placed at the front of the room. A student with attention difficulties will benefit from having access to an area in the classroom that is freer of distractions, such as an area behind a divider.

How do we know when to adapt the curriculum?

Changes in curriculum are based upon the needs and abilities of the student. Sometimes we assume that because the student has a disability, the curriculum must be adapted. In fact, many times no adaptation needs to be done at all for students with disabilities. It is important to begin with that assumption. Then, if it is clear that the student will need some support, the level and type of support should be considered.

Perhaps the student can participate in the same activity with the same materials and strategies but with different expectations. When preparing for a spelling test, perhaps the student with a disability will have fewer spelling words. If not, then perhaps the student may need different materials. Perhaps spelling words more relevant to everyday life would be appropriate for this student. Materials may include changes in the way students access information. For example, if the class is reading a story, a student with a disability may listen to it on a tape.

Sometimes a student's needs will best be met through participating in a similar activity. For example, when a class is writing an essay, a student with limited language ability who is unable to express him or herself with words can use a computer to select relevant pictures, or the student might cut and paste pictures from magazines into a journal book.

There may be times when participation in a class activity is not possible. For example, when the class is taking a paper and pencil test, and the student with a disability is not able to participate, it may be appropriate for the student to complete a different activity in a different location—provided the activity meets specific goals and objectives of the student's IEP.

Adaptations of activities can be viewed along a continuum, such as the one illustrated in Figure 3.5.

Figure 3.5   Continuum of Adaptations

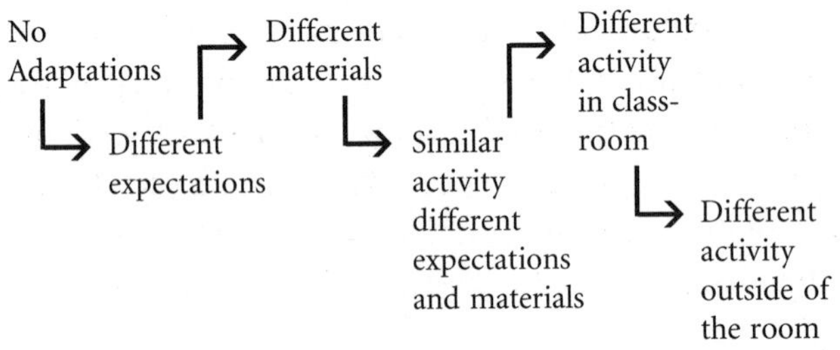

It cannot be stressed enough that it is essential to begin with the assumption that any student can participate fully in an activity. If we don't consider ways in which the student can participate in classroom activities without adaptation, we run the risk of teaching content that does not challenge students. Mastropieri & Scruggs (2000) suggest that before adapting a lesson, the goals and objectives for all students should first be considered. Then, those objectives upon which a student with a disability needs to focus on should be highlighted and adapted if necessary. And yet, simply because a student cannot master the stated class objectives, it is not clear that the student will not benefit from remaining in the class with different objectives or goals. Those objectives that may be unattainable for the student with a disability should also be noted. Before eliminating any objective for a student with a disability, adaptation of these objectives should be considered.

How do students with significant disabilities "gain access" to the general education curriculum?

Statewide curriculum standards must be addressed by all students. Connecting these curriculum standards with the learner's individualized needs can sometimes be a challenge, especially with students who have significant disabilities. It is important to first look at the essential questions of each curriculum standard (Kleinart & Farmer Kearns, 2001). The key, or central, question is, "What is at the heart of this standard?" To help us determine the "heart of the standard," considering the essence, or entry points, is helpful.

Figure 3.6 Definition of the entry points and the essence of curriculum standards.

Entry points
> Challenging, but achievable, goals for the student based on the Massachusetts *Curriculum Frameworks.*

Essence (of the standard)
> A summary of the key concepts, skills, and content outlined in a learning standard.
> From: *2002 Educator's Manual for MCAS Alternate Assessment,* Massachusetts Department of Education.

Consider this science standard: "Explain how air temperature, moisture, wind speed and direction, and precipitation make up the weather in a particular place and time." Entry points of the curriculum learning standards that have been modified for students with significant disabilities reflect lower levels of complexity and difficulty, while retaining the essential meaning (*essence*) of the standard. At the *essence* of this standard, students should be able to determine various components of weather in a given location, e.g., define weather for the day. *Entry points* to this standard may include reading temperature and precipitation charts and comparing the differences from day to day. More complex skills may be determining factors that are involved in hurricane development. So, while some students may be working on reading thermometers, others may be learning to read complex weather charts.

Using a math standard taken from the *Resource Guide to the Massachusetts Curriculum Frameworks for Students with Significant Disabilities* (Commonwealth of Massachusetts, 2001), this fundamental curriculum adaptation concept is exemplified in Figure 3.7.

Figure 3.7 Illustration of the breakdown of a standard for students not performing at grade level.

Learning standard: Represent, order, and compare large numbers (to at least 100,000) using various forms, including expanded notation, e.g., 853 = 8 × 100 + 5 × 100 + 3.		
Essence of the standard	Entry skills	Demonstration of the entry skills
• Manipulate numbers at a higher level by counting, writing, grouping, sorting, comparing, and ordering • Use a variety of numerical forms/classes • Recognize and use decimals • Understand and compare equivalent forms of decimals and fractions	• Identify parts of a whole (1/2, 1/4, 1/3, 1/8) written as a fraction • Split groups of objects into two, three, or four equal parts • Identify parts of each set of fractions in written format • Write money as decimals with dollars and cents	Dominique participates by making purchases with her peers. She selects items for purchase and indicates the amount needed by identifying the "next highest dollar" from the price given. A vertical number line provides Dominique with support so she can participate independently in this activity.

Figure 3.7 illustrates a direct link between a math standard and the math skills that Dominique can work on in the general education classroom. Dominique can work on these skills alongside, and perhaps with some support from, her "typical" peers. It is clear that, although Dominique is not addressing standards as they are written, she is given access to the standards. If Dominique were not in the general education classroom, such links might not be made between the instruction she is receiving and the general education curriculum.

How do we ensure that we are preparing students with disabilities to meet our society's expectations?

As we work toward reconciling individual student needs with the general education curriculum, we must also consider the expectations society has for students when they graduate. Students must be prepared to be as independent as possible in the community. For the most part, the general education curriculum *is* what society expects students to know as adults. Adhering to the frameworks, whether we are working toward the essence of them or modifying the benchmarks, will lead students to success as adults. In many states, passing the statewide tests and achieving a high school diploma is the ticket to that success.

At times, however, a student's needs may fall outside of the frameworks. Some students, even after a concerted effort to address the general education curriculum, may be unable to pass statewide testing as it is designed for the general student population. Yet these students do need the critical skills necessary to function as independent adults. For these students, when connecting with the general education curriculum, we must ask the question, "Why do they have to know this? Is it important for them to know this as adults?" Especially when students have reached their high school years, the general education curriculum may need to be modified to ensure that the functional skills necessary for independent living are addressed.

Looking again at Grace's activity/skills matrix in Figure 3.4, we see that one of the scheduled periods of her day is called "Vocational Skills." During this period Grace will prepare for jobs in the school or community. Any variety of jobs may be appropriate, such as working in the school store or cafeteria. It is important to consider jobs that are of interest to Grace. Some of the most important skills she will learn at any job will be getting along with others, following directions, and working independently. These are the skills that are most valued by employers. Job tasks can be trained—but if employees do not bring good social skills to the workplace, they will never succeed.

How do we ensure that high standards are maintained for all students?

Not only are all students now expected to be taught the same curriculum, but accountability for instruction is also mandated by IDEA. All students must participate in state-mandated, or "high stakes," testing. The reason these tests are referred to as "high stakes" is because high school diplomas are often contingent upon students passing the tests. Some students may participate in these tests through an *alternate* assessment—but it must be linked to curriculum standards. Any assessment must be designed to assess the student's progress toward meeting the general education curriculum. Just as there are many ways in which students can participate in the general education curriculum, there are also many ways in which they can participate in high-stakes assessment. Alternate assessments often look like portfolios that are organized according to state curriculum standards and present a collection of the student's work toward meeting these standards. In this chapter, we have presented ways in which teaching, learning, and assessment can be modified to allow full participation in meeting curriculum standards. If students are required to participate in assessments that test their knowledge of the general education curriculum, then they must be given the opportunity to learn the curriculum.

For many teachers, it is difficult to imagine how students with significant disabilities might benefit from being included in their classrooms when their needs may be very different from other students. We run a great risk of underestimating a student's ability if we automatically assume that he or she cannot learn what others are learning. Time and again many teachers have told us that the ability of students with disabilities exceeded the teachers' expectations. If we do not keep the bar high for all students, we will not be able to help them to achieve their full potential.

The utilization of the same curriculum benchmarks for all students ensures that teachers will strive to maintain high standards in their expectations. While many parents and professionals object to high-stakes testing of students with disabilities, the continued use of these tests for all students will ensure that all students will be challenged to the maximum extent possible.

Some teachers express concern that including students with disabilities in the classroom will result in a negative impact on the test scores of other students. As noted in chapter 1, the research shows that all students benefit from inclusion, and the performance levels of all students is strengthened by inclusive practices (Lipsky & Gartner, 1996; Peck & Staub, 1994).

Perhaps most importantly, as students with and without disabilities learn alongside each other, they develop the ability to understand and tolerate differences that will be one of the most important learning achievements in school. Many "typical" adults who have not benefited from growing up in inclusive environments do not understand, and may even be afraid of, individuals with disabilities. Certainly no one can argue against the need for more tolerance in today's society. Understanding the differences and challenges an individual with disabilities faces is a first step in understanding all differences of people in our society.

References

Garcia, J., & Rothman, R. (2002). Three paths, one destination: Standards-based reform in Maryland, Massachusetts, and Texas. Washington, DC: Achieve, Inc.

Halvorsen, A., & Neary, T. (2001). *Building inclusive schools: Tools and strategies for success.* Needham Heights, MA: Allyn and Bacon.

Individuals with Disabilities Education Act, 20 U.S.C. 1400 et seq. (1997).

Kleinart, H., & Farmer Kearns, J. (2001). *Alternate assessment: Measuring outcomes and supports for students with disabilities.* Baltimore: Paul H. Brookes.

Lipsky, D. K., & Gartner, A. (1996). Questions most asked: What research says about inclusion. *Impact on Instructional Improvement, 25*(1), 77–82.

Massachusetts Department of Education. (2001). *Massachusetts curriculum frameworks.* Malden, MA: Commonwealth of Massachusetts.

Mastropieri, M., & Scruggs, T. (2000). *The inclusive classroom: Strategies for effective instruction.* Upper Saddle River, NJ: Merrill.

Paulson, J., & Fognani-Smaus, K. (1997). *Understanding the IEP as a tool to access curriculum and instruction.* Paper presented at the second annual conference on: New Directions in Special Education: Preparing Today's Practitioners for Tomorrow's Schools.

Peck, C. A., & Staub, D. (1994). What are the outcomes for nondisabled students? *Educational Leadership 52*(4), 36–40.

Stainback, S., & Stainback, W. (1992). *Curriculum considerations in inclusive classrooms: Facilitating learning for all students.* Baltimore: Paul H. Brookes.

Tyler, R. (1969). *Basic principles of curriculum and instruction.* Chicago: University of Chicago Press.

Effective
Teaching Practices

What is different about inclusionary teaching from other ways of teaching?

It is our belief that instruction in an inclusive classroom should be the same as exemplary instruction in a classroom without students with disabilities. There are four key assumptions we make regarding teaching. The first assumption is that good teaching is based on the belief that all students can and do learn, and that all students belong in the general education classroom regardless. The second assumption is that good teaching is based on the fact that all learners are different, and therefore, instruction must be different and individualized for all students. The third assumption is that the curriculum should be student centered. Our final assumption is that *all* educators and *all* administrators are responsible for the education of *all* students.

When teachers believe that *all* students can and do learn, they are more apt to be accepting of students with disabilities in their classrooms. These teachers regard students with disabilities as members of the classroom community and include them in their planning. Effective teachers establish high learning and behavioral expectations for *all* students, and all teachers work with all students.

Classrooms today are as diverse as society. Students differ in race, ethnicity, gender, socioeconomic backgrounds, family structure, and learning styles and needs. In order to address this diversity in the classroom, instruction must be diverse. Teachers must employ a variety of teaching approaches and strategies. There are many teaching approaches and strategies that support the inclusion of students with disabilities and are also good teaching approaches for all students. These approaches and strategies will be discussed later in this chapter. First, we would like to take a look at strategies that provide more challenges to inclusion.

For many years, and even in some classrooms today, teachers teach and have taught by lecturing. So often we walk down the halls of schools, look into classrooms, and see students seated at desks in nice, neat rows with their books propped up in front of them reading along with the teacher, furiously jotting down notes as the teacher stands in the front of the room lecturing. This style of teaching is so contrary to what we know about how students learn, yet it continues to be utilized in many classrooms. It is almost impossible—if not completely impossible—for many students with disabilities, as well as those without disabilities, to participate meaningfully in this type of learning environment. They are not actively engaged in the learning activity. It is difficult to establish a sense of community in this classroom. The teacher is the "sage on the stage." Students are mere receptacles for the teacher's knowledge.

How would John, a student with an auditory processing problem, be able to participate in this type of learning environment? How would Jane, a student with cerebral palsy and limited fine motor control, be successful in this type of learning environment? How would Michael, a student with dyslexia, participate in this learning environment? Our belief is that it would be difficult for each of these students. It would also be difficult for many students without disabilities, whose learning style is not conducive to this type of teaching.

In an inclusive classroom, the teacher is the "guide on the side" rather than the "sage on the stage." Students work cooperatively, experiment with information and materials, and construct their own knowledge while the teacher guides them. Activities are structured so that students of all abilities can participate meaningfully. Heterogeneous groups of children work together. Students support each other and learn from each other. A variety of materials are used to teach a concept. Instruction is provided in a variety of ways, and students demonstrate learning in a variety of ways. Instruction is based on the students' abilities and needs. Learning is active, engaging, and relevant. Students are motivated to learn. Students communicate with, share with, and support each other. There would be a sense of community. All students would feel a sense of belonging.

Good teachers watch and observe students. They listen to the questions students ask and engage the students in finding the answers. Instruction is based on these observations and questions. The students are at the center of the curriculum. Decisions of what and how to teach are based on what the students already know and how the students learn best. Material or content learned is relevant to the students.

What teaching approaches support inclusion in the general classroom?

We support the notion that, while students with significant disabilities may require specialized instruction some of the time, for the most part, teachers' instruction in inclusive classrooms should not be any different than exemplary instruction in any general education classroom. Good teaching is good teaching for all. In our work in schools, we have seen inclusion at its best, at its worst, and everything in-between. We have found inclusion at its worst in what we see as "traditional" classrooms—classrooms where, as described earlier, teachers lecture and do not utilize a variety of instructional approaches or instructional materials. On the other hand, we have found inclusion at its best in classrooms where teachers employ a variety of different instructional approaches and materials and where special educators and regular educators work together for the good of all students.

As stated previously in this chapter, there are many good teaching approaches that support inclusion. We see these approaches as good teaching pedagogy for all students and they should be part of instruction in all general education classrooms. If these strategies are utilized in the general education classroom, not only do many students with disabilities benefit, but many typical students will benefit too.

What are these good teaching approaches? We feel there are several good teaching approaches that can be incorporated into instruction that support all learners in the general education classroom. Cooperative learning is one approach that allows many students to participate in the same activity at different ability levels. Differentiated instruction addresses a variety of unique learning needs and styles. Peer tutoring allows students to work together and to demonstrate, improve, and utilize their strengths as learners and individuals. Incorporating Gardner's (1998) theory of multiple intelligences in teaching provides opportunities for students to learn and demonstrate their talents and skills in different ways. Thematic units incorporate a variety of integrated activities on a specific theme. Teaching with thematic units offers learners many opportunities to learn and be successful. Each one of these strategies will now be discussed in the context of meeting the needs of students with disabilities in the inclusive classroom.

Cooperative learning is an excellent teaching strategy that allows students with a wide range of abilities to be successful. In cooperative learning arrangements, students work in small, heterogeneous groups with their peers to achieve a shared academic goal rather than competing against, or working separately from, their classmates (Salend, 2001). David Johnson & Roger Johnson (1999), define five elements of cooperative learning: 1) positive interdependence (a sense of sink or swim together), 2) face-to-face promotive interaction (helping each other learn, applauding successes and efforts), 3) individual and group accountability (each of us has to contribute to the group achieving its goal), 4) interpersonal and small group skills (communication, trust, leadership, decision making, and conflict resolution), and 5) group processing (reflecting on how well the team is functioning and how to function better).

When carefully designed and orchestrated, cooperative learning arrangements offer many learning opportunities for all students. Students assume roles in cooperative learning arrangements. Traditional roles may include facilitator, recorder, reporter, timekeeper, and materials gatherer. Roles are typically assigned according to students' strengths, offering each member of the group the chance to be successful. Other roles can be created based on the educational goals of individual members. For example, a student with severe disabilities might have the goal of pointing to pictures to communicate. In a cooperative math group, this student's role may be to point to manipulatives as the other members of the group count the manipulatives. Could our student, Jane, with cerebral palsy, be able to participate in this environment? We believe she would be and could be very successful. The Activity Virigule Skills Matrix presented in chapter 3 (Figure 3.4) provides an illustration of planning to address an individual student's goals across academic classes. Cooperative learning within the general education classes provides an ideal context for collaborating with other professionals. A speech and language specialist might work collaboratively with the classroom teacher to structure a cooperative learning project that could promote strategies to elicit optimal language during the activity. An occupational therapist might support the teacher by suggesting how to select materials and where to position them for the most effective utilization, and a physical therapist might brainstorm with the teacher to identify the best possible seating arrangements.

The use of cooperative learning arrangements in inclusive classrooms help foster the acceptance of students with disabilities. A student with severe disabilities may be working on a social goal, i.e., making eye contact when communicating with others. In a cooperative group this can be addressed through the pairing of students to work together or in small groups. A natural social context is created for the student to practice this skill. Another social goal for a student may be to learn how to take turns. Designing an activity that requires the student to participate in a cooperative learning arrangement and take turns allows the student the opportunity to practice this goal. Other members of the group model turn-taking for the student with disabilities and provide natural reinforcement when the student is successful.

During a lesson on ancient civilization, students may be grouped heterogeneously to work on a project. Michael, our student with dyslexia, may be a good artist, so he may assume the role of illustrator in this cooperative learning arrangement rather than be asked to read and gather information. Our student John, with auditory processing problems, might possess strong oral communication skills, so he may be the reporter. Another student with strong writing skills may be the recorder, etc. Opportunities for different ways of participation are available. Each member of the group is able to participate in the learning activity in a way that best addresses his or her strengths, allowing him or her to learn the information.

Another teaching approach that we find highly effective in supporting all learners is *differentiated instruction.* Differentiated instruction addresses the diverse needs and learning styles of all students. In differentiated classrooms, students drive the curriculum. Teachers design content instruction based upon students' ability levels and understanding. It is not based on a certain page at the front of a curriculum guide (Tomlinson, 1999). In differentiated classrooms, teachers know that curriculum and instruction must be powerful, relevant, and engaging. They then ask how that curriculum can be modified so that it adheres to high standards, yet allows each learner the opportunity to acquire the skills and knowledge needed for the next phase of learning. These teachers understand that there are many commonalities among learners but that there are also essential differences that make each learner an individual.

Differentiating instruction is merely the tailoring of one's teaching and the learning environment to the needs of each student. Differentiation is based on several assumptions. They are as follows:

- Students differ in experience, readiness, interest, intelligences, language, culture, gender, and modes of learning.
- To maximize the potential in each learner, educators need to meet each child at his or her starting point and ensure substantial growth during each school term.

- Classrooms that ignore student differences are unlikely to maximize potential in any student who differs significantly from the "norm." This is an issue even in "homogeneous" classrooms where student variance is inevitably great.

- To ensure maximum student growth, teachers need to make modifications for students rather than to assume that students must modify themselves to fit the curriculum. In fact, children do not know how to differentiate their own curriculum successfully.

- Best-practice education should be the starting point for differentiation. It makes little sense to modify practices that defy the best understanding of teaching and learning.

- Classrooms grounded in best-practice education, and modified to be responsive to student differences, benefit virtually all students. Differentiation addresses the needs of both struggling and advanced learners. It addresses the needs of both students for whom English is a second language and students who have strong learning-style preferences. It addresses gender differences and cultural differences. It pays homage to the truth that we are not born to become replicas of one another (Tomlinson, 1999, p. 24).

Teachers must look at students as individuals. It is almost as if each student has an individual educational plan. We frequently hear, "How can I do that when I have 25 students in a class?" and "I am just one person!" We call on Abraham Lincoln for our response, which is that you cannot meet all the needs of all the students all the time—but if instruction is varied you will meet some of the needs of all the students some of the time. Tomlinson (1999) recommends modifying a curricular element only when 1) you see a student need, and 2) you are convinced that modification increases the likelihood that the learner will understand important ideas and use important skills more thoroughly as a result. Without varied instructional approaches and modifications in the regular classroom, there are some students whose needs will never be met.

How can teachers differentiate instruction for students? Differentiated instruction can be: a) the manner in which instruction is delivered, b) modifications to instruction, c) adaptations to instruction and the environment d) accommodations, and e) classroom organization and/or structuring the learning environment. It is a new way of looking at learners. It is recognizing that no single approach to teaching will work for all students and not one or the same environmental conditions are beneficial to all students.

There are a variety of ways instruction can be delivered. The traditional form of delivery is lecture, and there is a place for this in the inclusive classroom. Some students learn best auditorily and need to hear information presented. But, as a teacher, one must ask the question, "What can I do for those who have difficulty learning this way or who are less likely to retain information this way?" This might be the case for learners with auditory processing problems. The following is an example of how a social studies lesson can be differentiated for these learners.

Mr. Smith plans a lecture for his fifth-grade class on the Civil War. This is the introductory lesson, and he feels the students need some background information prior to reading the information he has gathered. He thinks about the students in the class and remembers that Jack and Jill have difficulty processing information they hear. He wants to be sure that they have the same base of knowledge as the rest of the students in the class. He lists the accommodations he can offer to students. His list is as follows:

- provide a copy of the lecture to these students with key vocabulary words omitted (cloze procedure)

- have lecture notes on transparencies or PowerPoint presentation

- provide a graphic organizer for students (see Figure 4.1)

- provide carbon paper so a peer can take notes for each student

Mr. Smith can make these "tools" available to all students who choose to use them. Many students without disabilities will also find them useful in learning.

But what about the individual with a more severe disability? How can that student participate in Mr. Smith's social studies class? Again, teachers must consider the needs of the student and the objectives in the IEP (discussed in chapter 5). Goals and objectives for the student are not always academic in nature. In other words, it may not be the social studies concept that is important for the student to learn, but a skill that will help him or her become more independent. Fred, who has a severe disability, is working on understanding "cause and effect": e.g., if I do *X*, *Y* will happen. He is learning the very basic concept that when his body moves, it can have an impact on objects in the environment, and he can control this action. What better

Figure 4.1   Graphic organizer for instruction on the Civil War.

The Civil War

Who?: ————————————   When?: ——————————
————————————

Causes:

1)

2)

3)

Effects on history:

1)

2)

3)

way is there to have Fred practice this than when Mr. Smith is doing his PowerPoint presentation? Fred can press a key on the computer keyboard or use the mouse to move to the next slide when cued by Mr. Smith.

Oftentimes in schools, knowledge is obtained through reading. Teachers will ask students to read chapters in books, articles, and/or handouts to learn new information. Students who learn through visual modalities will be successful. But what about the individuals with a reading disability, or the individuals who have difficulty retaining information obtained visually? The following is an example of how a teacher may differentiate instruction in a science lesson for these learners.

```
     Mrs. Wilson is preparing a lesson on photosynthesis.
She has a handout that explains the process to students.
She decides that she will have the students read the
handout to learn about the process of photosynthesis
because she has had success in using it with previous
classes in previous years. In thinking about the stu-
dents, she remembers that George and Mary have diffi-
culty processing information visually. She decides that
she must include some adaptations or accommodations to
support their learning. She plans the following:
```

- prior to reading the handout, she will conduct a K-W-W-L (K = What do I know, W = What do I want to know, W = Where can I go to find it, and L = What did I learn), on photosynthesis with the students (see Figure 4.2)

- during the reading of the handout, she can pair each student with a peer to read

- she can have the reading on tape for the students to listen to as they read the handout

- she can have the members of the class read the handout aloud to the group

- after reading the handout, she can create a semantic web or concept map on photosynthesis on transparencies as well as have copies for students to fill in (see Figure 4.3)

These "tools" can be available to any student who feels the need to use them. But, again, the questions must be asked, "What about the individual with a more severe disability? How can that student participate in Mrs. Wilson's science lesson?" Keeping in mind our expectations for the student and the student's goals and objectives, there are certainly ways he or she can be included in this lesson. For instance, an objective for Sara may be to learn to identify the students in her class by name. She may be selected to choose the students to read aloud by pointing to pictures of classmates and saying their names.

Figure 4.2 K-W-W-L Chart.

K(now)	W(ant)	W(here)	L(earn)

Figure 4.3 Graphic organizer for teaching photosynthesis.

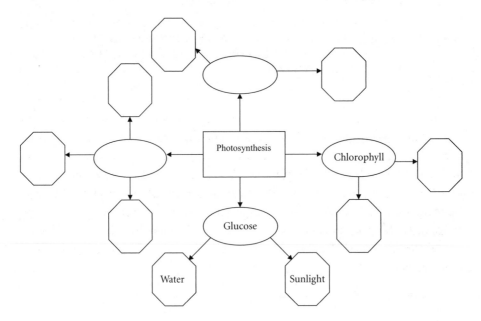

Reading is one of the most critical skills taught in schools today. How can teachers differentiate reading instruction? The Guided Reading Approach developed by Fountas & Pinell (1999) is an instructional approach to the teaching of reading that naturally differentiates instruction. Guided reading provides instruction to small groups of students who are at the same developmental reading level. They read from leveled texts (see Fountas & Pinell, 1999, for more information on leveled text) and are provided reading instruction at their entry level. Leveled books are categorized by the difficulty of the text, the number of words on the page, the regularity of words, and the number of syllables in words.

Books are classified into three types: *independent* (meaning one can read the book independently with 96% accuracy and make meaning from or comprehend the text), *instructional* (meaning one can read this book with instruction or scaffolding from the teacher and make meaning from or comprehend the text), and *difficult* (meaning that one would struggle to read this book and make meaning from or comprehend even with instruction). This approach to reading allows all students to be successful, since they are expected to read text that they can read. They are not being asked to read text that is too difficult for them.

Instruction in guided reading is determined through careful observation and assessment of students' reading behaviors. After gathering the necessary information, teachers group students and plan instruction based on their developmental level. Once again, the students drive the reading instruction and curriculum, not the teacher. Instruction focuses on reading for meaning, problem solving new and more difficult words, and working with phonics all in the context of the text.

Just as there are effective strategies for teaching reading, there are also effective strategies for teaching mathematics. Students with auditory, visual processing, and/or reading disabilities may have difficulty with mathematics instruction also. As well, many students without the aforementioned disabilities will struggle with mathematics. The term "dyscalculia" is sometimes used to describe the difficulty students have in understanding and doing mathematics. How can a teacher differentiate mathematics instruction for these learners as well? The following is an example of a differentiated mathematics lesson.

Ms. Marshall is planning to introduce the concept of fractions, decimals, and percentage to 23 students in her third-grade class. She has a handout that lists the fractions 1/1, 1/2, and 3/4. Next to each fraction is a circle to demonstrate the fraction. (See Figure 4.4) While reflecting on the needs of the learners in the class, she realizes the following:

1. seven students do not understand fractions,

2. three students will need to be paired with a peer for assistance,

3. five students will need to hear an explanation,

4. two of the students do not seem to get or retain mathematics concepts, and

5. the remainder of the students seem to get mathematics without any difficulty, no matter how it is presented.

Ms. Marshall decides that she will introduce fractions to students by sharing apples with the class. She will ask students if they want a whole (1) apple, a half (1/2) of an apple, or three quarters (3/4) of an apple. She will ask students to choose the correct piece of apple based on what fraction they chose. She will build their prior knowledge and background information. Then, during the explanation, she will use the overhead transparency with the whole, half, and three-quarter pieces of circles to demonstrate the concept. She will give students paper to make their own set of fraction bars or fraction circles. At this time, she will pair students to work together. Finally, she will have students solve and create real-life problems with fractions. Students will be allowed to use their own set of fraction bars or a fraction calculator (a calculator that computes fractions).

Because Ms. Marshall incorporated varied teaching and learning materials and methods of delivering instruction, it is highly likely that most of the 23 students in the classroom will be successful.

Figure 4.4 Transparency used by teacher to introduce fractions to class.

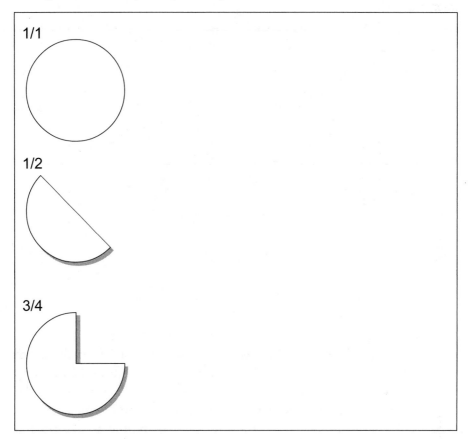

Again, let us consider the individual with a more severe disability. How can that individual participate in Ms. Marshall's mathematics lesson? Ronaldo, a third-grade student with a severe cognitive disability, is in Ms. Marshall's class. She wonders how she will include him in this lesson. She reads the objectives on his IEP and decides Ronaldo will be able to work on matching (in this lesson it will be matching shapes), a skill Ronaldo has been practicing. She thinks about how she might do this and comes up with the following template, Figure 4.5 (actually it is just Figure 4.4 reformatted):

Figure 4.5 Template for students with disabilities to use to match shapes of fraction pieces.

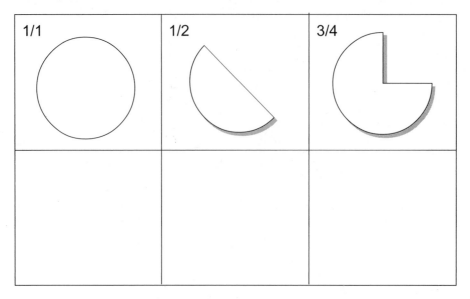

Ronaldo is given several examples of each shape to match to the shapes on the template. There may be a special education teacher in the room coteaching with Ms. Marshall, so that at any time someone can be checking in to see how Ronaldo is doing and offering support when necessary. She also seats Ronaldo near a peer whom she knows will understand the concept and lesson with little difficulty and who can then provide assistance to Ronaldo if necessary.

Designing work centers in the classroom allows teachers the opportunity to differentiate instruction. A work center is an activity aligned with the general education curriculum, i.e., math activity, writing activity, etc. A heterogeneous group of students work together to complete the activity. The work is designed to address all ability levels. For example, a language arts skill being worked on in a fourth-grade class may be homophones (words that sound the same, are spelled differently, and have different meanings, i.e., in/inn). After conducting a shared reading of a story, the teacher may design an activity for a work center that requires students to revisit the story and find as many homophones as they can in the story. Students make a list of the words they find. After finding as many words as they can, students then put the word pairs into a sentence. An example would be "I stayed *in* the *inn.*" Next, the students can illustrate their sentence. A book can be made for the classroom.

Expectations for each student will be different according to ability level. Some students will find more homophone pairs than other students, some students will only find the homophone pairs, and some students will use more sophisticated words in sentences and draw more elaborate illustrations. Some students may find pictures to represent a homophone pair rather than illustrating it. See Fountas & Pinell (1999), *Guided Reading: Good First Teaching for All Children*, for more on work centers.

Not only do teachers need to provide different ways for students to learn, but they must also be sure to keep students motivated to learn. A task that is moderately challenging to one student may be extremely challenging to another student and not at all challenging to yet another student. Tasks provided to students in the classroom must vary in complexity and challenge for students to continually learn. Work centers assist in motivating and challenging students of all abilities.

For the student with disabilities, in the classroom where various instructional approaches are employed and various modifications are made, success is certainly much more likely. If a student's academic goal is to sequence events in logical order, the teacher would design opportunities for the student to practice this skill throughout the day in activities such as reading (sequencing pictures), social studies (creating a time line), math (utilizing a number line to solve problems), etc.

Students who learn in different ways and who bring different talents and interests to school enjoy, and thrive in, differentiated classrooms. Students with disabilities benefit from classrooms that offer differentiated instruction because these classrooms offer opportunities for a wider range of students. Differentiating instruction is not a difficult thing to do, but it does take time and effort. If done well, however, the time and effort used will be well worth the results that are reaped.

Peer tutoring, another useful teaching method, is a form of cooperative learning. In peer tutoring, students "tutor," or assist, one another in learning new skills. Strengths and areas of need usually determine the pairing of students. For instance, a student who does well in math may be paired with a student who has difficulty in math. After instruction by the teacher, the students work together to complete an activity, which requires the application or extension of material already covered. In no way should peer tutoring be one student providing instruction on a newly introduced skill or concept to another student. The teacher provides the instruction, and peer tutoring is used when students are practicing a new skill or applying new knowledge.

Peer tutoring increases student learning and fosters positive attitudes toward school (Longwill & Kleinert, 1998). By helping others in the learning process, students also help themselves. Teaching a concept or skill reinforces the learning of it. (One remembers 90% of what they teach.) Peer tutoring can also support the acquisition or refinement of social skills. Students learn responsibility as well as increase their self-concept.

Designing activities and learning materials that address Howard Gardner's (1993) theory of *multiple intelligences* are necessary in inclusive classrooms. Gardner believes that individuals possess strength in seven (if not more) intelligences. The seven intelligences are logical-mathematical, musical, visual-spatial, verbal-linguistic, interpersonal, intrapersonal, and bodily-kinesthetic. Students with disabilities, like students without disabilities, possess strengths in one or more of these different intelligences. When allowed to learn through a variety of strategies and when allowed to demonstrate what they have learned through different modes and outcomes, students with and without disabilities have an opportunity to be successful.

Therefore, material and information presented in a variety of methods fosters success for students with disabilities in an inclusive classroom. Using music (to learn multiplication facts), movement (acting out the parts of a plant), art (to show the life cycle of a butterfly), etc. are all nontraditional ways of fostering learning for many students.

In addition to asking students to write a research paper and/or essay on what they have learned, students sometimes need a variety of options to demonstrate what they know and how they know it. For example, after completing a unit on the Civil War, students may be given the following options to demonstrate what they have learned:

- Create a poster
- Write a report
- Write a song
- Create a collage
- Develop a conversation between two prominent figures
- Design a brochure
- Give a speech as a prominent figure during the Civil War
- Design a comic strip
- Create an alphabet book
- Suggest your own project and consult with teacher

The use of *thematic* or *interdisciplinary units* supports the inclusion of students with disabilities in the general education classroom. The thematic approach addresses many subjects through one theme or topic (Kochhar, West, & Taymans, 2000). Oftentimes, students with disabilities are placed in environments that rely quite heavily on the use of verbal skills. These students tend to learn best by doing, creating their learning through construction of knowledge. Thematic units typically incorporate hands-on learning activities, hence allowing students with and without disabilities to participate meaningfully.

The use of *technology* in the classroom also supports the inclusion of students with disabilities. Technology extends far beyond the use of the computer. There are a variety of electronic devices that can be used by students with intensive disabilities to communicate. There are devices, such as the Kurzweil 3000, as well as software programs that can read material to students. Portable electronic communication devices provide "voices" for individuals without the ability to speak. There are switches (joy switches, pads, and ball switches) and touch screens for computers (an overlay for the computer screen in which the student makes choices by touching an area on the screen instead of using a mouse or the keyboard) that allow students with intensive disabilities to use the computer. There are books on tape. The technological resources are abundant and should not be ignored, especially if they create an opportunity for an individual with disabilities to be successful in an inclusive environment.

Technological advances have also made possible a new approach to teaching, learning, assessment, and curriculum design referred to as *Universal Design for Learning* (UDL) (CAST, 2002). Building on universal design concepts generally associated with architecture, CAST has drawn on new technologies and new brain research to develop a new paradigm. The fundamental premise behind UDL is that "a curriculum should include alternatives to make it accessible and appropriate for individuals with different backgrounds, learning styles, abilities, and disabilities in widely varied learning contexts..." (CAST, 2002). UDL is rooted in the key principles of differentiated instruction, but the focus is more on the development of materials that incorporate digital multimedia which are designed to allow for individualization in response to student needs and/or learning styles. A fundamental premise behind UDL is that rather than constituting a separate category, students with disabilities fall along a continuum of learner differences.

Universally designed materials use technology to incorporate four techniques which are generally accepted as best practice in teaching: 1) providing multiple examples, 2) highlighting critical features, 3) providing multiple media and formats, and 4) supporting background knowledge (Rose & Meyer, 2002). For example, students at different stages of writing proficiency might be supported through the use of various multimedia resources, such as story templates, "clip" media, drawing programs, and digitized images. A key to making UDL truly useful for the students is to remain focused on the *learning goal*—the use of these tools is a means of achieving that goal—not an end in itself. Numerous examples of designing and using universally designed materials are available at the CAST Web site (http://www.cast.org/udl/).

Although there are many elements necessary for inclusion to be successful, it is our belief that the teachers and their teaching are critical to successful inclusion of students with disabilities. Effective and informed teachers never shy away from including students with disabilities. They welcome all students. These teachers intuitively know how to teach. The pedagogy and strategies they employ are what all students need to learn.

In addition to good teaching approaches, there are other specialized teaching programs that make it possible for students with disabilities to learn in the general education classroom. *Direct instruction* is an approach that provides students with modeling and explicit skill instruction. There are many specialized programs for instruction in reading and mathematics. Orton-Gillingham and Wilson Reading are two reading programs that utilize direct instruction. Both of these programs are multisensory, and students learn through visual, auditory, and tactile/kinesthetic methods, with an emphasis on phonics. Touch Math is a tactile approach to teaching mathematics and offers success to students whose preferred mode of learning is kinesthetic. Direct instruction is also used in this mathematics program.

Just as students learn better through different modes and different instructional approaches, they also learn better under different environmental conditions. Some students cannot concentrate on learning if they are too cold or too hot. Some students find bright lights distracting, and others may fall asleep in lights that are too dim. Some students need to move more frequently than others. Noise can bother some students, but can be quite necessary for other students to learn. What about the students that read better in the afternoon? What about the students who are easily distracted? Teachers should consider all these environmental conditions. Daily schedules can reflect differentiation. Reading can be taught at different times on different days. Seating arrangements for different activities should be carefully considered.

Appendix B provides a list of additional strategies that have been found to be helpful in supporting inclusion. Most of the time, however, the best approach is generated from problem solving to find creative solutions to the challenges students face in the classroom.

I'm overwhelmed! Do I have to do this alone?

The previous section of this chapter discussed what we feel are the exemplary teaching practices which are most likely to support inclusion. Does the classroom teacher do this alone? Can good teaching practices alone support inclusion? Our answer to both questions is, "No!" Exemplary teaching alone will not make for successful inclusion. What else, then, is needed? We feel there are several other elements which are necessary to make inclusion work.

Special educators are crucial to the success of inclusion. Their expertise can be used in a variety of ways. The most effective way we have found is through a coteaching model. In a coteaching model, a special education teacher and a classroom teacher work together in harmony, in the classroom. Responsibility is shared, teaching is shared, planning is shared, and paper work is shared.

As "partners," each teacher has the opportunity to learn from the other. The special educator is knowledgeable in the assessment of needs, modifications, and adaptations for learning and can share this knowledge with the classroom teacher. The classroom teacher, on the other hand, has more expertise in the general education curriculum and can share this expertise with the special educator. Together the pair can brainstorm ideas and can design and implement lessons and activities, which will meet the needs of all learners.

We have seen models of coteaching where there are two teachers per classroom throughout the day. But many of us know that this model is costly and not common in many schools. Ideally, we feel this is the most likely model to promote successful inclusion. The next best option is for teachers to coteach particular content areas, i.e., reading/language arts, science, math, and/or social studies. Schedules can be designed so that special educators can be available to coteach at the times they are most needed (when classroom teachers and students need the support). Whether or not coteaching is possible, it is critical that time be scheduled into the day for special education and general education teachers to meet in order to problem solve and plan effective learning experiences.

In addition to special educators supporting inclusion in the general education classroom, related service personnel (physical therapist, occupational therapist, and speech and language pathologist), Title I staff, and paraprofessionals, or "tutors," may be utilized. These professionals can collaborate with teachers to design instruction and adapt the learning environment and curriculum for the diverse needs of learners.

Staff and teaching strategies are the two most important elements contributing to the success of inclusion. Along with these, teachers need resources and materials. They need professional development, the appropriate materials to teach with, and the recognition for what they do for students.

There are many components that contribute to the success of inclusion of students with various disabilities. In today's classrooms, it is not likely that you will find all elements present. Does that mean, then, that students cannot be successfully included? We say, "Definitely not!" Through creativity and collaborative problem solving and the availability of resources and materials, teachers and support personnel can create learning environments in which all students have the opportunity to participate and learn.

Chapter 5 will address one of the most important tools in designing instruction for students with disabilities—the Individualized Educational Program. This document presents a comprehensive picture of students with disabilities and a plan to meet their needs.

References

CAST Universal Design for Learning. (n.d.). Retrieved August 26, 2002, from http://www.cast.org/udl/.

Fountas, I. C., & Pinell, G. S. (1999). *Guided reading: Good first teaching for all children.* Portsmouth, NH: Heinemann.

Gardner, H. (1993). *Multiple intelligences: The theory in practice.* New York: Basic Books.

Johnson, D. W., & Johnson, R. T. (1999). *Learning together and alone: Cooperative, competitive, and individualistic learning.* Boston: Allyn and Bacon.

Kochhar, C. A., West, L. L., & Taymans, J. M. (2000). *Successful inclusion: Practical strategies for a shared responsibility.* Upper Saddle River, NJ: Merrill.

Longwill, A. W., & Kleinert, H. L. (1998). The unexpected benefits of high school peer tutoring. *Teaching Exceptional Children, 30*(4), 60–65.

Rose, D. H., & Meyer, A. (2002). *Teaching every student in the digital age: Universal design for learning.* Alexandria, VA: ASCD. (Full text also available at http://www.cast.org/teachingeverystudent/ideas/tes/.)

Salend, S. J. (2001). *Creating inclusive classrooms: Effective and reflective practices.* Upper Saddle River, NJ: Merrill.

Tomlinson, C. A. (1999). *The differentiated classroom.* Alexandria, VA: Association for Supervision and Curriculum Development.

Chapter
5

The Individualized Educational Program: Ensuring Students' Needs Will Be Met

What is an "IEP"?

An Individualized Educational Program (IEP) is a document designed by a team consisting of parents, school professionals, and the student when appropriate. Every child who receives special education and related services must have an IEP. An IEP delineates learning strengths and difficulties and describes the educational program necessary to meet the needs of the individual child. The IEP has been described as "the cornerstone of a quality education for each child with a disability…" (OSERS, 2000, p. 3).

Why do we use IEPs?

Prior to 1975, when IEPs became mandated by federal law PL 94-142, students with disabilities were not guaranteed any educational programs. Some students did not attend school at all, and others did not receive an appropriate educational program. There was no accountability for monitoring and evaluating students' progress each year. The IEP serves as a type of contract between the school, the student, and his or her parent(s) that delineates an agreed-upon educational program and a means of evaluating that program.

Is any student who is experiencing learning problems eligible for an IEP?

If a student is experiencing learning difficulties, he or she can be referred to a prereferral team for a review of the student's current performance and to determine any interventions that may assist the student to succeed in the general education classroom. Rather than providing special services directly to the child, prereferral generally involves an indirect form of service, where the classroom teacher is provided with resources or supports to assist the child (Ysseldyke, Algozzine, & Thurlow, 2000). The prereferral team typically consists of the student's teacher, another classroom teacher or two from the building, the special education teacher, and the building principal. But depending on the child's problems, the school's philosophy, and the resources available in the school, a prereferral team may also include specialists, such as a school counselor, social worker, nurse, or school psychologist. School districts use a variety of names for prereferral teams, including Teacher Assistance Team (TAT), Student Support Team (SST), and Child Study Team (CST). School districts also vary in their approaches to prereferral intervention, but there is increasing emphasis on the use of collaborative problem-solving strategies and the importance of training team members to work collaboratively (Whitten & Dieker, 1995).

Regardless of the approach taken, it is the goal of the prereferral team to determine the nature and severity of a student's problems and to design an intervention that the classroom teacher can utilize to meet the student's needs. Many times, a change in instructional strategy that can be easily implemented by the classroom teacher can lead to success for a student (Mastropieri & Scruggs, 2000). In a survey of prereferral intervention assistance teams in Illinois, the following strategies were identified as being the most successful: 1) behavior management, 2) peer tutoring, 3) individualized instruction, 4) small group instruction, 5) consultation with professionals, 6) teacher/student conferences, 7) teacher observations, and 8) cooperative learning (Whitten & Dieker, 1995, Table 2).

If, after attempting interventions designed by the prereferral team, the student is still not successful, he or she may be referred for a comprehensive educational evaluation. The purpose of the evaluation is to determine if the student has a disability and is in need of special education services. Parent consent is required before the child can be evaluated. The educational evaluation should address the unique needs of the student who has been referred for an evaluation. McLoughlin & Lewis (2001) suggest the development of an individualized assessment plan (IAP). This plan is not a formal or required document, but is a guide to ensure that all necessary evaluations are completed and that all team members are working collaboratively. The IAP must address the reason the student was referred for assessment, focus on areas relevant to education, and result in information that will be useful in developing an appropriate education program. If, for example, a student's primary area of difficulty is in reading, formal and informal assessments—as well as observations of the student during reading classes—should be conducted. Typically, a special education teacher will conduct these assessments. A speech pathologist may be asked to conduct a speech and language assessment to determine if the reading problem is language based. A school psychologist may be asked to conduct a psychological evaluation of the student to determine his or her cognitive abilities.

A student who, after having been evaluated, is found to be a "child with a disability," as defined by IDEA, is eligible for special education and related services (OSERS, 2000). Appendix A provides an excerpt from IDEA regulations that lists and defines those disabilities which could result in a student being eligible for an IEP.

If a child does qualify for special education services, an IEP team must meet within 30 calendar days to develop an IEP. In addition to the services of a special educator, the child's individualized program may include related services. As listed in IDEA, related services include (but are not limited to):

- audiology services
- counseling services
- early identification and assessment of disabilities in children
- medical services
- occupational therapy services
- physical therapy services
- speech and language therapy services
- rehabilitation counseling services
- recreation
- school health services
- social work services
- transportation

How is an IEP developed?

Once the assessments are conducted and a disability has been determined, a team consisting of parents and professionals is convened to develop the IEP. The child's parents are critical members of the team, and every effort must be made to help parents understand the purpose of the meeting and to facilitate their attendance. As specified in IDEA, the IEP team must include the following members:

1. The parents (or surrogate parent) of the child;

2. At least one regular education teacher of the child (if the child is, or may be, participating in the regular education environment);

3. At least one special education teacher, or if appropriate, at least one special education provider of the child;

4. A representative of the local education agency (LEA) who:

    i. is qualified to provide, or supervise the provision of, specially designed instruction to meet the unique needs of children with disabilities;

    ii. is knowledgeable about the general curriculum; and

    iii. is knowledgeable about the availability of resources of the LEA;

5. An individual who can interpret the instructional implications of evaluation results, who may be a member of the team described above;

6. At the discretion of the parent or the school, other individuals who have knowledge or special expertise regarding the child, including related service personnel as appropriate; and

7. The student, if age 14 or older, must be invited. Younger students may attend if appropriate (34 CFR 300.344).

At the IEP meeting, assessment results are shared and goals and objectives for the student are developed. Instructional strategies, accommodations, and/or modifications are delineated to meet identified needs. The development of the IEP should be a team effort, with each member contributing and consensus reached on every decision. Once it is written, the parents have the right to accept or reject their child's IEP. If rejected, the process may be mediated in a number of ways, with the ultimate goal being the development of a document that will meet the student's needs, and one that can be agreed upon by all.

What does an IEP include?

The Individuals with Disabilities Education Act (IDEA) delineates the required components of a student's Individualized Educational Program (IEP). This document, which is developed collaboratively by parents and professionals who work with a student, must include the following:

1. A statement of the student's present level of educational performance, including the student's strengths and how the disability affects the student's involvement and progress in the general curriculum.

2. A statement of annual goals, including benchmarks or short-term objectives related to meeting the child's needs in a way that enables the student to be involved in and progress in the general education curriculum.

3. The IEP must identify how a child's other educational needs, such as how a student communicates with others and/or how the child's behavioral issues affect the student's learning or the learning of others.

4. A statement of the special education and related services and supplementary aids to be provided to the child.

5. A statement of any modification or supports to assist the student's learning and to help the child progress in the general education curriculum and in meeting individual goals.

6. An explanation of the extent, if any, to which the child will not participate with nondisabled children in the regular class.

7. A statement of how the child's progress will be measured and communicated to parents, at least as often as other students receive grade reports, such as report cards (Federal Register, 1999).

The seven items listed above are required by IDEA to be a part of the IEP, but the law does not specify the format of the IEP. The actual format varies from state to state, and some states have additional requirements.

What does an IEP look like?

To illustrate what the components of the IEP might look like, we will provide two examples: one of a student with a mild/moderate disability, Keisha; and the other of a student with a severe disability, Miguel. IEP forms, formats, and requirements vary from state to state, but these examples will illustrate the key components that should be included on any student's IEP.

Student's Name: **Keisha**

Primary diagnosis: **Reading Language Disability**

Student's present level of educational performance

Keisha is 11 years old and in the fourth grade in school. She is a very cooperative student who works well with peers and adults. She is always eager to do her work in school and will ask for help when needed. She has difficulty following directions and staying focused on tasks when they are challenging for her.

Reading: Reading instruction is provided to Keisha using materials at a lower grade level. She has difficulty in decoding and with word recognition. Her difficulty in deciphering words and word meaning interferes with her comprehension, which is at an early-third-grade level.

Mathematics: Keisha enjoys math and is functioning at grade level. At times, she has difficulty following directions and understanding new concepts.

Other subject areas: Keisha performs well in other subject areas, including science and social studies. She does encounter difficulty, however, when extensive reading is required to attain subject matter knowledge.

Annual goals, benchmarks, or short-term objectives

GOAL 1: Keisha will decode one- and two-syllable words with consonant-vowel-consonant (CVC) patterns using all vowel sounds and will decode one- and two-syllable words with vowel digraphs.

Benchmark/objectives:

Given a new vowel digraph, Keisha will demonstrate her understanding of the sound by correctly pronouncing words containing digraph syllables in the CVC pattern with 9 out of 10 pronunciations correct.

Given words with open-syllable, vowel-consonant "e" combinations (e.g., canine), Keisha will recognize the pattern and correctly pronounce the words utilizing the pattern with 9 out of 10 pronunciations correct.

Keisha will read a controlled reading passage that contains closed syllables, open syllables, and vowel-consonant "e" in various combinations with no more than 15 errors for every 100 words.

GOAL 2: Given reading material at the third-grade level, Keisha will demonstrate her knowledge of comprehension and story grammar by finding the main idea, sequencing events, and answering factual and inferential questions.

Benchmark/objectives:

Given three different paragraphs, Keisha will determine the main idea and at least two supporting details for each.

Given five factual questions after reading, Keisha will correctly answer all questions related to the story.

Given a reading passage with descriptive words and phrases, Keisha will interpret the materials to find the author's true meaning on the passage.

A statement of the special education, related services, and supplementary aids to be provided to the student:

Reading instruction utilizing a structured, direct instruction approach.

A statement of any modification or supports to assist the student's learning and to help the child progress in the general education curriculum and in meeting individual goals:

Accommodations:

Books on tape

Alternative reading material at the second-grade level

Preferential seating near teacher or peer tutor

When working within content areas, alternative reading at her level should be provided, or partner her with a peer reader

Oral direction should be repeated and clarified

Reduce the workload in challenging areas and allow for more time to complete work

Modifications:

Tests in content areas will be read to Keisha

Grade on content rather than on mechanics or spelling

How do other educational needs affect the student's learning or the learning of others?

Keisha has no significant behavioral problems, but her occasional off-task behavior when faced with challenges does occasionally interfere with her ability to complete work. Keisha may need reminders to stay on-task, and encouragement/reinforcement when she is able to make progress on difficult tasks.

A statement of how the child's progress will be measured and communicated to parents:

In addition to a report card, quarterly progress reports will be written to address IEP goals and objectives. These reports will be given to parents in conference or delivered to the home via mail during scheduled marking periods.

As one can see from the IEP excerpts for Keisha above, the IEP flows from the student's strengths and needs that result from the child's disability. Goals provide a global identification of priorities for Keisha, and the benchmarks/objectives break down, and more clearly delineate, what the targets should be for Keisha. The IEP provides teachers with a list of appropriate accommodations and modifications that have been agreed upon by the team. The IEP includes very specific criteria for meeting the objectives, and it describes the process that will be used in reporting results.

Keisha's goals and objectives are well within the parameters of the general education curriculum. The accommodations and modifications identified can easily be delivered in the general education classroom. Now let's consider Miguel, who has more significant cognitive and physical disabilities and whose goals may not be as clearly linked to the general education curriculum.

Student's Name: **Miguel**

Primary diagnosis: **Cerebral Palsy with significant motor and cognitive difficulties**

Student's present level of educational performance

Miguel is 11 years old and in the fifth grade. He is very social and enjoys being around people, greeting them with smiles and laughter. Miguel is unable to orally communicate and uses a picture-symbol system to make his needs and interests known. He is nonambulatory and relies on others to push his wheelchair. He continues to require substantial verbal and physical prompts to maneuver his battery-powered wheelchair (left-hand control).

Reading/Language Arts: Miguel uses Mayer Johnson symbols (a commercially developed picture-symbol communication system). He points to symbols in order to communicate. He has an approximately 50-word/symbol vocabulary, consisting mostly of nouns and a few adjectives (e.g., big, hot, thirsty). Without symbols, Miguel has a sight-word vocabulary of approximately 15 words.

Mathematics: Miguel is inconsistent in his ability to indicate more/less. He is currently working on matching number cards with picture cards showing the same number of objects. Miguel has a 70% success rate in matching cards from 1–5, and a 40% success rate with cards from 6–10.

Other subject areas: Miguel attends science and social studies classes with his peers every day. During these classes he continues to work on his language goals of pointing to pictures on his communication board, following simple directions and pointing to objects and pictures in the context of the lesson (e.g., when the class was working on identifying the parts of a flower, Miguel pointed to pictures of flowers in groups of pictures of many objects). He occasionally requires verbal prompting to initiate this communication.

Annual goals, benchmarks, or short-term objectives

GOAL 1: Miguel will increase his word/symbol vocabulary to over 100 words across environments.

Benchmark/objectives:

Miguel will increase his vocabulary by 5 words/symbols per quarter in each of his major subject areas, for a total of 20 words per quarter.

Miguel will pair two picture symbols to communicate, such as noun/verb and adjective/noun.

GOAL 2: Miguel will use a motorized wheelchair to travel from class to class, and within classrooms.

Benchmark/objectives:

Miguel will travel from one room to an adjacent room with paraprofessional support nearby, utilizing the switch with only verbal prompts.

Miguel will independently maneuver his wheelchair within each classroom.

Miguel will travel distances of 100–200 ft from his current location, with no more than one instance of physical assistance and occasional verbal prompting.

A statement of the special education, related services, and supplementary aids to be provided to the student:

Miguel will receive physical and occupational therapy support one hour weekly (each) to assist the special education staff in maintaining current physical status and to assist Miguel in his use of the wheelchair.

Additional time will be allowed for travel to classes, as Miguel improves his wheelchair mobility skills.

A statement of any modification or supports to assist the student's learning and to help the child progress in the general education curriculum and in meeting individual goals:

Mayer-Johnson symbols will continue to be used, paired with the written word.

Augmentative communication device, such as Speak Easy, to orally state pictures when Miguel points to them.

Boardmaker™ software to assist with expansion of communication board.

How do other educational needs affect the student's learning or the learning of others?

Miguel's excitement when new people enter the room can be disruptive. He should be given warnings when interruptions are anticipated and reminders to remain quiet when possible interruptions are known. Reinforcement should be given when he remains quiet and greets people appropriately (e.g., a wave or smile).

Miguel's goals and objectives are not subject-matter specific. Rather, they are targets for him to aim for across all environments. He can address objectives in communication and mobility if he is working on science, math, at recess, or in the library. He will be far more motivated to communicate and travel with typical peers than he would be with other students who are also unable to communicate and ambulate on their own. His IEP serves as a guide for all teachers across all environments to help Miguel address his special needs while learning the curriculum alongside his peers.

Figure 5.1 below shows the relationship between the general education curriculum and the IEP for students with mild or moderate disabilities.

Figure 5.1 The relationship between the general education curriculum and the IEP.

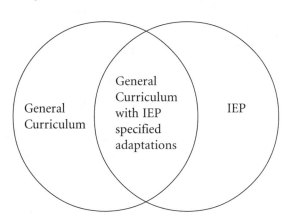

Figure 5.1 illustrates that, with only a few exceptions, the IEP provides access to the general education curriculum. The IEP does not need to repeat or redefine the general education curriculum. The area of overlap in Figure 5.1 represents the skills, strategies, and services the student needs to access the general education curriculum. Occasionally, the student will be learning separate curriculum components mandated by the IEP (e.g., activities of daily living, vocational skills). At other times, a student will be learning the general education curriculum with no accommodations or modifications. But mostly, the student will access the general education curriculum with accommodations or modifications identified in the IEP. The more significant the disability, the more time the student may spend on a separate curriculum; therefore, there will be less overlap between the IEP and the general education curriculum—but *all* students *must* access the general curriculum at some point during their school day.

How is an IEP used in daily instruction?

A review of the components of the IEP illustrates the fact that this is a very detailed document providing comprehensive information about the student's abilities, needs, and goals, as well as describing appropriate interventions for the teacher to utilize in the course of daily instruction. The document, while necessary to delineate what will be done to address the student's needs, is typically more detailed than is necessary or useful for teachers working with a child on a daily basis. To address the cumbersome nature of the IEP, some districts use a "Snapshot IEP." The Snapshot IEP provides a brief summary of the most important information contained on the student's IEP. It serves as a quick reference to help the teacher ensure that he or she is meeting the student's needs on a daily basis. Typically, the Snapshot IEP is only about one page. A sample Snapshot IEP form, developed by Goor & McCoy (1993), can be found in Figure 5.2.

There are many versions of the Snapshot IEP, but we particularly like Goor & McCoy's version because it provides a framework for culling important information from the IEP into a useful organizational tool for the classroom teacher. Identifying "organizational strategies" to help the student approach a learning task is something a teacher should be reminded of on a daily basis. The section on "cautions" will prove useful in helping the teacher avoid situations that will lead to a student's shutting down or perhaps acting out in frustration. One addition to this form could be a section on behavioral strategies for students whose behavior is difficult in the classroom. The format of the Snapshot IEP may vary depending on the student's individual needs. The goal of the document is to briefly highlight key elements for teachers to refer to when working with a particular student. The form we have provided serves as a sample; however, modifications can be made to the form to meet the needs of any student, teacher, or school district. As students get older, we also recommend that they participate in the writing of the Snapshot IEP, or at least be very familiar with their own Snapshot IEP. This document can serve as a tool, or reference guide, to enable students to advocate for their own individual needs.

Figure 5.2 The Snapshot IEP.

CONFIDENTIAL
SNAPSHOT IEP for <u>Mark - Grade 2 (age 8)</u>
Date _____

Present Level of Functioning: (Reading, Communication, Social Skills, Motor Skills, etc.) • Mark has difficulty maintaining attention to task (5 minutes maximum) • Reading skills are just merging (CVCC words in familiar patterns) • Math skills are at single-digit addition and subtraction level, but he is eager to engage in math activities • Penmanship is poor with some reversal of letters • Frustrated easily and may cry if presented with too great a challenge • He has difficulty picking up on the social nuances with other children and has few friends • His speech is hesitant and he has difficulty finding the "right words"	

Key Annual Goals:
1. To increase length of attention on structured tasks to 10 minutes
2. To improve reading skills so that Mark is able to late 1st grade materials
3. To increase self-advocacy skills so that he initiates asking for assistance (without crying) when presented with a challenging task (9 / 10 opportunities)
4. To increase social skills so that he interacts with peers within structured classroom and outside activities without adult assistance.

Learns Best:
- When paired with other students
- With visual supplements to auditory directions
- When he does not feel too much pressure to give complicated oral responses
- With manipulatives to supplement or replace paper and pencil tasks

Adaptations: Environment/Curriculum:
- Provide ample positive reinforcement for success
- Reading material with pictorial cues
- Seat next to student likely to provide support
- Allow use of computer or Alphasmart for some written assignments

Motivators:	**Organization Strategies:**
• Computer games • Verbal praise from peers as well as teacher • Time to draw	• Preview schedule changes • Allow time for transitions to allow him to prepare • Chunk assignments
Assessment:	**Cautions:**
• Evaluate on % correct out of items completed • Review vocabulary before test	• Low frustration level • Provide feedback privately • Don't ignore raised hand!

Input Received from:

Student _____   Parent _____

Teachers _____   Others _____

_____   _____

Adapted from Mark Goor & Elizabeth McCoy (1993)

What role does the IEP play in linking the student's needs, the curriculum, and society's expectations?

The Individualized Educational Program (IEP) becomes an important tool in linking the three key information sources in Tyler's curriculum development model presented in chapter 3. In developing effective, truly individualized IEPs, we must first consider the student's current as well as future needs. If we are not thinking ahead to future environments where students will live and work, we run the risk of teaching them nonessential skills. Questions to consider are:

- What will he/she be doing next year?
- What will he/she be doing in 5 years?
- What will he/she be doing in 10 years?
- What will he/she be doing as an adult?
- What will the student need in school this year to help him/her achieve the vision for his/her future?

These questions ask us to consider what society will expect from the student, and what services, if any, will be necessary and/or available for the student. While the answers to these questions may evolve over time, it's important to keep asking these questions with each new IEP. And as the child gets older, his or her personal preferences will play a greater role in shaping the IEP.

The IEP team develops goals and objectives to meet the vision for the student's future. The IEP development process asks us to consider a student's needs, as well as their areas of strength. The impact that the disability has on the student's ability to progress in the general education curriculum must also be addressed. Ultimately, the IEP needs to specify exactly what is expected of the student over the next year, and exactly what teachers and other school personnel need to do to help the student meet those goals.

What if the student is evaluated and determined to have a disability, but does not qualify for special education services?

As described in chapter 1, all students with disabilities are protected by Section 504 of the Rehabilitation Act. Those students with disabilities who do not qualify for special education services, and who therefore do not have an

IEP, may qualify for general education accommodations necessary for them to receive an appropriate education. These are students whose disability is not found to adversely affect their educational performance, but whose disability does substantially limit one or more of their major life activities. Examples of conditions which might qualify a student for accommodations through Section 504 include attention deficit hyperactivity disorder (ADHD), chronic medical conditions, physical or sensory impairments, and temporary medical conditions (Livovich, 1996). For example, a child with diabetes might need to have frequent snacks, or could require daily trips to the health office for blood testing or insulin injection, while a student with ADHD may require preferential seating and peer tutoring. Students found to be protected by Section 504 and needing accommodations are eligible for a Section 504 plan, which may be given another name (e.g., Alternative Learning Plan, Accommodations Plan, etc.).

Unlike an IEP, a Section 504 plan does not have specific content requirements and does not need to be reviewed on an annual basis. Classroom teachers, however, need to be knowledgeable about the content of a student's Section 504 plan. "All staff (including all teachers) *must* follow the Plan otherwise they violate the student's rights and the law…" (Livovich, 1993, p. 34). In many districts, the format of the Section 504 plan might be compared to the Snapshot IEP in that it is short and focused primarily on what the child needs to succeed in the general education environment. Two very different sample Section 504 accommodation plans are included in Appendix C.

Classroom teachers should also know the identity of the district or school-based Section 504/ADA coordinator. Like the prereferral process, the development and implementation of Section 504 plans is considered to be a function of general education rather than of special education. Ultimately, the goal of both prereferral interventions and Section 504 accommodations is to ensure that an individual child is receiving whatever supports and accommodations are needed to succeed in the general education classroom. The general education curriculum is not being altered, and fundamental curricular expectations are not being changed, but the classroom teacher is usually the individual playing the central role in making the necessary accommodations for the child. Blazer (1999) provides a very useful framework for teachers to use in developing accommodation plans for students and also provides a plethora of sample accommodations, which fall into three categories: physical, instructional, and behavioral accommodations.

References

Blazer, B. (1999). Teacher tips: Developing 504 classroom accommodation plans—A collaborative, systematic, parent-student teacher approach. *Teaching Exceptional Children, Nov/Dec, 28–33.*

Federal Register. (1999). Washington, DC: U.S. Government Printing Office.

Individuals with Disabilities Education Act, 20 U.S.C. 1400 et seq. (1997).

Goor & McCoy (1993). Snapshot IEP: Manual of ideas for accommodating students' unique learning needs in general education classrooms. Paper presented at the annual conference of TASH. Boston, Massachusetts.

Livovich, M. P. (1996). *Section 504 of the rehabilitation act of 1973—Implementing access to a free appropriate education: A teacher's manual.* Chesterton, IN: Author.

McLoughlin, J., & Lewis, R. (2001). *Assessing students with special needs.* Upper Saddle River, NJ: Prentice Hall.

Mastropieri, M., & Scruggs, T. (2000). *The inclusive classroom: Strategies for effective instruction.* Upper Saddle River, NJ: Prentice Hall.

Office of Special Education and Rehabilitation Services (OSERS), U.S. Department of Education. (July 2000). *A Guide to the individualized education program.* Jessup, MD: U.S. Department of Education, Editorial Publications Center.

Whitten, E., & Dieker, L. (1995). Intervention assistance teams: A broader view [Electronic Version]. *Preventing School Failure, 95*(40), 41–45.

Ysseldyke, J. E., Algozzine, B., & Thurlow, M. L. (2000). *Critical issues in special education (third edition).* Boston: Houghton Mifflin Co.

Making It Work

Chapter 6

Advocating For Change:

Building on the Belief That All Students Will Benefit from Inclusive Education

What is the current status of inclusion?

The degree to which inclusion is implemented in schools today is very much defined by the schools themselves. The reality is that school communities, even some which are in the same district, are implementing the philosophy of inclusion in different ways. There are other realities cited by Bartlett, Weisenstein, & Etscheidt (2002) that dictate how inclusion is being implemented across the country. They include the following:

1. Inclusion is no longer a choice—it has been legally mandated;
2. There have been successes that have resulted in greater respect and understanding among diverse groups of people;
3. There have been failures due to inadequate planning and support that have had a negative impact on inclusive philosophy; and
4. When implemented properly, inclusion is successful for students and staff.

Inclusion is not the latest fad in educational trends. It is not a strategy, and it is not just a place in the regular classroom. It is a philosophical belief that *all* children belong to *our* school community and that they belong together. As noted in chapter 1, this belief is supported by the U.S. Constitution and was upheld through such litigation as Brown v. The Board of Education (1954), Oberti v. The Board of Education (1993), and Sacramento

v. Holland (1994). No amount of strategies, creative ideas, detailed lesson plans, or curricula will be effective unless professionals and parents of students with disabilities embrace the belief that all children can learn together. Without a strong philosophical foundation and a belief in inclusive education, the moment a problem arises we will be more likely to say, "See, it doesn't work. Let's pull the student out of the general education classroom and put him or her someplace where his or her needs can be better met." If, however, we truly believe in inclusive education, when problems arise we will examine the situation carefully and ask, "What creative strategies can we use? What supports are needed to assist the student and teacher in this situation?"

Many of the "baby boomer" generation—the generation that staffs our schools in substantial numbers—were taught in schools without any children with disabilities. If students with disabilities were in the building, they were often placed in classrooms in the school basement, or at the end of the hall, where they were less likely to disturb others. It is almost always difficult to visualize or accept a concept that runs contrary to our own experiences. Thirty years ago, a prediction of dwindling postage stamp sales due to instant E-mail communication would have been met with incredulity. Similarly, it is difficult to imagine all students achieving success in general education classrooms when we have been taught/observed/learned that students with disabilities should be taught in small groups, with "special" strategies, and with other students having similar needs.

How do we convince others and ourselves that inclusive education is "the way to go?"

Changing belief systems in others and ourselves is a most challenging endeavor. Mara Sapon-Shevin (1992) recommends that we begin by examining our own understanding, values, and beliefs about diversity. We should consider our life experiences and our interactions, if any, with people from other races, cultures, and/or people with disabilities. Sapon-Shevin (1992) suggests that by examining our past experiences and the ways in which we learned about people whose backgrounds are different from our own, we can grow to understand our own biases. Understanding ourselves and how our biases developed will help us to understand the prejudices we see in others. Through this understanding, we can think about ways to break down the barriers. If, for example, we learn that teachers in a school have very limited experience or knowledge about students with disabilities, presenting them with information is a first step in breaking down the barriers.

Sharing literature or videotapes about students who have been successful in inclusive classrooms can begin to build acceptance. Hearing students with disabilities and their families tell their own stories is an effective way to help others to understand the challenges that have been met and overcome by students with disabilities. Visiting schools where inclusion can be seen in practice, and where inclusive thinking is inherent in their philosophy, is a very powerful means of changing negative attitudes and beliefs.

As noted in chapter 4, much of the "individualized, special instruction" that had been reserved for students with disabilities in the past is currently accepted as best practice for all children. Today's best practices are grounded in the notion that all children learn differently and have diverse learning styles, skills, and intelligences. This way of thinking about teaching and learning promotes a school environment that can benefit all students.

How can we advocate for change?

So how do we convince all educators to embrace inclusion? As mentioned in the introduction to this chapter, most of today's professionals grew up with the paradigm that students with disabilities are best served apart from the mainstream of school and community. Students with more significant disabilities were educated in institutions or separate day schools. Today's educators probably do not have any prejudices against people with disabilities, but they may simply believe that students with disabilities learn best with others having similar needs. They cannot fathom what a student with a significant disability, who is functioning at a much lower level than the "typical students," might gain from being in the general education classroom.

This lack of knowledge and understanding of the potential of people with disabilities—or the possibilities that might be gained from learning in inclusive classrooms—serves as a roadblock for inclusionary practices in schools. Unless professionals truly believe that inclusion is best for students with and without disabilities, they will continue to be quick to dismiss the possibilities for students who present challenges to the general education teacher. Likewise, if a student does not readily gain from an inclusionary setting, someone who does not fully support inclusionary practices might be quick to say it isn't working, rather than working to find a solution. All children present challenges to general education teachers at some point during their school years. When challenges arise, we convene parents and all those who work with the student throughout the day to problem-solve on how to address these challenges.

Students with disabilities deserve the same opportunity. Rather than jumping to the conclusion that inclusion isn't working, we must ask, "How *can* it work?" Much of the resistance from teachers comes from their lack of training to deal with students who have disabilities. Scruggs & Mastropieri (1996) conducted a study of teacher attitudes toward inclusion, and found that many teachers were resistant to having students with disabilities in their classroom because they were not given sufficient support. Teachers cited their own lack of training, insufficient resources and materials, the lack of support personnel, planning time, and large class sizes all as obstacles to successful inclusionary practices. Dev & Scruggs (1997) found that teachers who had received some training had more positive attitudes toward inclusive teaching than teachers who had not had such preparation. Professionals should advocate for their own professional development and preparation in teaching in inclusive environments. As has been stated, effective inclusionary practices are built on what we know to be effective teaching practices. In order to shift our thinking about how students with disabilities can benefit from inclusive teaching, most teachers will need to have some guidance to put this philosophy into practice.

What do teachers need to be effective inclusionary teachers?

Effective inclusionary teachers are known for their creativity and for their openness to problem-solving strategies and curriculum adjustments to meet the needs of all learners. Chapters 3 and 4 identified some of the effective practices that inclusionary teachers utilize toward ensuring that their classrooms meet the needs of all learners.

In addition to the teaching tools identified in those chapters, there are certain attributes of teachers who are effective in inclusive settings. Peterson & Beloin (1998) identified characteristics of elementary and middle school teachers that are necessary for inclusive practices to be effective. Their combined lists yield the following qualities for effective inclusionary teachers:

1. Have the right attitude
2. Are team players
3. Are willing to change and take risks
4. Generally care about *all* kids
5. Are comfortable with different modes of instruction
6. Are trained and comfortable in modifying and adapting instruction

7. Are knowledgeable about all things related to special education (Speech, ADHD, etc.)

8. Are able to talk to and work with colleagues

9. Know their stuff

10. Understand the difference between learning and schooling

11. Know a lot about everyday informal assessment

12. View content holistically

13. Say, believe, and operationalize that all kids can learn

14. Teach differently rather than more/faster/harder/longer

As one reviews the items above, it appears that this list presents a comprehensive criteria for identifying teachers who will succeed in inclusive classrooms. It is clear that it isn't always what you know, but how you view the task that is equally, if not more important. As we have stated repeatedly in this text, inclusion is a philosophy that must be embraced. The absence of that philosophy in guiding educational decisions will lead to failure.

Successful school inclusion requires the support of teachers, parents, administrators, and students. As described in chapter 2, these are the primary stakeholders in the educational process. Each group has something to gain when the philosophy of inclusion is embraced and put into practice. And just as each group has something to gain, each group can play an important role in the movement toward more inclusionary practices in a school or community. In the following section, possible actions are identified for teachers, parents, students, and administrators.

What can teachers do to help other teachers?

Teachers who support inclusion and who hope to see more inclusionary practices in their schools are in a very powerful position to influence others in embracing the philosophy. There are a number of ways this can be achieved:

a) *Serve as a role model*

Teachers who support inclusive education should follow the adage "Seeing is believing." When challenged by others who believe that including students with disabilities in the general education classroom will not be effective for either these students or their classmates, teachers can best respond by showing how it can and does work in their own classroom. Inviting parents and colleagues into the classroom to observe successful inclusionary practice provides evidence that is difficult to refute. Discussing the successes both in various meetings and in the teachers' room can spread the enthusiasm. Teachers can vounteer to be a member of the prereferral team in their building to support other teachers in addressing the needs of students who are having difficulty.

b) *Start small*

Teachers with whom we have worked often note, "I support an inclusionary philosophy, but my principal/colleagues are very much opposed to such an approach. What can I do?" Perhaps the worst approach that advocates for inclusion have taken is to target the top-level administrators and confront them with a need for comprehensive change. Some teachers have taken this approach and have informed the administrators in their district of the legal requirements. Telling and forcing someone to embrace any philosophy is certain to lead to resistance. Starting in small ways to show successes and build on each success will more likely lead to changes in attitudes and practice.

Instead of targeting a student or a group of students for inclusion in the general education classroom for an entire day, a smaller goal may be more appropriate. Perhaps the target should be a class where a student is most likely to succeed. Classes with teachers who employ the strategies outlined in chapter 4, such as cooperative group activities or direct instruction, will be more conducive to including students with disabilities than classrooms where teachers employ a lecture-type teaching style.

Teachers who are encouraged to work with students with disabilities should be provided the necessary supports. Without the necessary supports, the effort is likely to fail and the small steps taken will become the last. In the ideal situation, the general education and special education teachers work collaboratively to design instruction to meet the needs of all students. With each successful lesson, confidence and acceptance of the teachers will grow, and an inclusionary philosophy will become much easier to embrace and build upon. Yet, few schools have the ideal situation, and creative resource use may be necessary to get started. Sometimes it takes brainstorming and thinking outside the box to make optimal use of the resources you already have (Giangreco, 1993).

What can a parent do?

If knowledge is power, then parents can best equip themselves by learning about inclusion and studying the research and legal precedents. Many of the references used in this book are great resources. The Lipsky & Gartner (1996, 1996a) article that discusses the increased academic achievement of students with disabilities who are placed in general education classrooms presents some very powerful arguments for inclusion. Several resources are targeted specifically toward parents and can provide a wealth of information. The most comprehensive of these is the Parent Advocacy Coalition for Educational Rights (PACER) Center. PACER's Web site (www.pacer.org) provides links to training information, legislative updates, and links to other centers and community groups. The PEAK Parent Center in Colorado (www.peakparent.org) is known for their publications and resources in inclusive education, as is the Federation for Children in Massachusetts (www.fcsn.org). These centers, and/or their links, may provide parents with the names of people who can serve as advocates at team meetings, and perhaps more importantly, many of these organizations help parents to connect with other parents who face similar challenges.

There is one area in which parents can be certain that they have the expert knowledge—the needs, wants, hopes, desires, and abilities of *their* child. While it is sometimes very difficult to combat the negative attitudes and biases of some professionals toward students with disabilities, it is imperative that parents remind professionals of their expectations and hopes for their child.

What can students do?

Students with disabilities can and should play an active role in designing their educational program. IDEA '97 mandates that from age 14, students must be invited to participate in their own IEP team meetings. Parents and professionals must make certain that the student's voice is heard at these meetings. For some students, speaking out for themselves in front of a gathering of professional adults can prove to be too much of a challenge. These students might be more comfortable sharing their needs and feelings prior to the meeting. This can be done by meeting with parents and a few professionals with whom they are most comfortable—or some students might prefer to prepare a written statement of their needs and concerns.

Students without disabilities can become involved in promoting inclusive educational practices. They can serve as peer tutors for students with disabilities, helping with assignments, or helping others to organize their assignments. They can facilitate transitions from one environment to another. They can be included in the problem-solving process. Students without disabilities who are able to work alongside students who have disabilities will greatly benefit from these experiences. As adults, they will become natural advocates to promote inclusion in schools and communities. Perhaps if all students learned in inclusive communities today, we would have such increased knowledge and understanding of disabilities that there would be no need for advocates in the future.

What can administrators do?

Goor, Schwenn, & Boyer (1997) have noted five core values that educational administrators should have in order for a successful inclusionary environment to be created. These core values include a belief that:

1. all children can learn
2. all children are accepted as part of the school community
3. teachers can teach a wide range of students
4. teachers are responsible for all students
5. principals are responsible for all students in the building (pp.134–135)

As much as we have stressed that teachers serve as role models in implementing inclusion, so too must the administrators. Goor, Schwenn, & Boyer (1997) emphasize this point, noting that modeling a positive attitude and expectation for collaboration is key for administrators of effective schools. If an administrator demonstrates through all of his or her interactions with staff, students, and parents that all children in the school are full members of the community, it will be embraced by the school. It has been our experience that in schools where the administrator is not supportive of inclusion, it is unlikely to succeed. Administrators must make it clear—through word and deed—that all students belong. When administrators suggest that when students cannot be successfully included they will be sent to another setting, it is less likely that school personnel will do all that they can to successfully include that student.

Administrators must also provide leadership. They should engage their staff in creative problem solving, and they should participate in the process. Creative problem solving includes:

- finding a clear definition of the problem
- developing hypotheses about why the problem exists

- brainstorming toward possible solutions
- implementing the solution
- evaluating the implementation (Giangreco, Cloninger, Dennis, & Edelman, 2002)

All of these steps are critical for the process to succeed. When administrators bring together a staff that is open to new ideas, they can generate many possibilities that make impossible situations seem solvable. Without evaluating any attempts made toward problem solving, we have no means of determining our successes and learning from our mistakes.

Several years ago we worked with a group of teachers who found that one of their greatest obstacles toward creating an inclusive environment was finding time to work together. They needed time to develop and adapt curriculum, to creatively problem solve to meet the needs of students, and to develop ways in which they could create a community of learners. Utilizing the creative problem-solving process, they were able to identify over 100 ways in which they could utilize their time and find meeting opportunities across the day. These teachers amazed themselves with the number of possibilities the creative problem-solving process generated!

Administrators must also provide their staff with in-service training and technical assistance. Teachers and all staff should be assisted in conducting a self-assessment of their own skills and attitudes about inclusion. This will help to determine what professional development is needed. Access to journals and articles should be provided as a means of helping teachers understand inclusive philosophy and practices. One effective tool in helping teachers and staff toward creating a vision for inclusion in their school is to encourage them to visit schools where inclusion is successful. Seeing can be a means of believing, and opportunities to speak with staff who have already been through the process of designing an inclusive school can prove very helpful. If possible, it is especially useful if staff can visit more inclusive schools within their own district.

Where does a staff begin in implementing inclusion in their school?

Moving a school or a school system to one that is based on an inclusionary philosophy is a systemic issue. Administrators, teachers, parents, students, and other concerned parties must come together to collaborate in the design and implementation of an inclusive philosophy in their school. Again, there is no prescription for how to make it work, but there are key ingredients in a process that should be followed. These ingredients are outlined in Figure 6.1 below, and a more detailed description of each step follows.

Figure 6.1 Effective ingredients of inclusionary practices.

Necessary Ingredients in Implementing Inclusionary Practices:

- Planning
- Assessment
- Roles may need to be redefined
- The schedule can be changed
- Professional development must be part of the implementation plan
- Collaboration among team members
- "Right supports"
- Building a sense of community
- Involving students in the collaboration process
- Learn from the challenges
- Celebrate accomplishments

If any initiative is to be effective, *planning* must be the first step. All stakeholders should be involved—students, parents, teachers, administrators, and perhaps community representatives. Sufficient time must be provided for planning (Hobbs & Westling, 1998). That, of course, is easier said than done with the busy schedules of today's society. In order for inclusion to be effective, it must be seen as a priority. If implementing inclusion is a priority, time must be built into the schedule. Staff who stay after their required hours must be compensated appropriately.

Part of the planning process is *assessment*. A school must assess its strengths and areas of need. For example, when considering staffing and how staff will be used to implement inclusion, the following questions should be asked:

- What staff are available?
- How can current staff be used more effectively to fill areas of need?
- Where will more staff be needed?
- How can schedules be adjusted to support the appropriate staff?

Once these questions are answered, *roles may need to be redefined.* Perhaps the paraprofessional who has demonstrated effective teaching in the classroom should not be assigned recess duty to allow for more time to support students in the inclusive classroom. Perhaps *the schedule can be changed* to allow for the teaching of reading across the day so that the special education teacher can be freed up to support students struggling with reading in more classrooms. Similar questions should be asked about the physical environment and the resources available. While engaged in questioning and creative problem solving, it is essential that the primary goals be kept in mind. For example, before exploring ways to free up time for collaborative planning, be sure that you can articulate exactly how that additional time will be used.

The lack of training and preparation has been mentioned as one of the obstacles to inclusion. *Professional development must be part of the implementation plan.* A needs assessment should be conducted to determine staff training needs. As the staff implements inclusionary practices, ongoing support throughout the year will be needed to help them problem-solve their way around obstacles they encounter.

At the heart of inclusive practice is *collaboration among team members.* It is the bringing together of all staff to work toward meeting the needs of all students. In order for collaboration to occur, time must be allotted for communication to take place. Meeting time should be scheduled into the week just as any subject matter is scheduled. Without time to work together, instruction will be disjointed, teachers will not feel supported, and inclusion will fail.

The question is often asked, What are the *"right supports"* to promote effective inclusion? The answer to that question is, "Whatever it takes." Implied in that answer is the fact that there is no one answer to the question that can be stated for every school and for every situation. As schools work toward developing an inclusionary model, each school, its culture, its staff, its students, and its resources, is different. The school staff needs to examine its student population, determine the supports needed for every student to be successful, and then assign the appropriate resources. Supports may include paraprofessionals, therapy services integrated into the regular school program, peer supports, and assistive technology (Lipsky & Gartner, 1996b).

In addition to possible changes in instruction, schedules, roles, and materials, the most pervasive change that needs to take place is that of *building a sense of community.* Educators should build—into every day—opportunities for everyone to participate fully. Classroom activities should be modified so that every student has a possibility of contributing in ways that help them to accentuate their strengths and address their goals. Respect and appreciation of differences should be noted with every opportunity (Shaffner & Busewell, 1996).

Villa & Thousand (1992) stress the importance of *involving students in the collaboration process.* Villa & Thousand note that involving students in decision making and problem solving creates a community of active learners and gives them valuable tools for the future. We have often used students to help problem-solve around curricular issues. Ask students how they think activities can be more participatory or meaningful, and you may be surprised by their responses (Giangreco, 1993; Giangreco, Cloninger, Dennis, & Edelman, 2002). Their creativity is not hampered by any preconceived notions of how learning should take place.

A final and ongoing step that must be mentioned is the need to *learn from the challenges* and *celebrate accomplishments* (Shaffner & Busewell, 1996). Rather than getting discouraged by problems that arise and perceived failures that occur, these should be viewed as opportunities for the staff to learn for the next time if a similar situation arises. If challenges are to be pondered, accomplishments should be celebrated. Any new initiative in a school is hard work, and successes should be noted to serve as a foundation and energy source for further growth.

How long does it take for a school to implement an inclusive philosophy?

There is no typical time line for a school to follow when implementing an inclusive philosophy. The important thing to remember is that the process should begin as soon as possible. Far too much important learning time will pass if faculty waits until they feel that all the pieces are together. All of the pieces will never be together, and there will always be many competing demands on your time and resources. It is a process that will evolve and change as the students and staff in a school likewise change. With each day that passes, students miss opportunities to understand each other, respect each other's differences, problem-solve around issues that they face, and learn how to live in a community of diversity.

References

Bartlett, L., Weisenstein, G., & Etscheidt, S. (2002). *Successful inclusion for educational leaders.* Upper Saddle River, NJ: Merrill Prentice Hall.

Brown v. Board of Education of Topeka, 347 U.S. 483, 74 Sup. Ct. 686. (1954).

Dev, P. C., & Scruggs, T. E. (1997). Mainstreaming and inclusion of students with learning disabilities: Perspectives of general educators in elementary and secondary schools. In T. E. Scruggs & M. A. Mastropieri (Eds.). *Advances in Learning and Behavioral Disabilities, Vol. 11*, pp. 135–178. Greenwich, CT: JAI Press.

Giangreco, M. F. (1993). Using creative problem-solving methods to include students with severe disabilities in general education classroom activities. *Journal of Educational and Psychological Consultation, 4*(2), 113–135.

Giangreco, M. F., Cloninger, C. J., Dennis, R., & Edelman, S. W. (2002). Problem-solving methods to facilitate inclusive education. In J. S. Thousand, R. A. Villa, & A. I. Nevin (Eds.). *Creativity and collaborative learning: The practical guide to empowering students, teachers, and families* (pp. 111–134). Baltimore: Paul H. Brookes.

Goor, M. B., Schwenn, J. O., & Boyer, L. (1997). Preparing principals for leadership in special education. *Intervention in School and Clinic, 32*(3), 133–141.

Hobbs, T., & Westling, D. (1998). Promoting successful inclusion. *Teaching Exceptional Children, 31*(1), 46–51.

Lipsky, D. K., & Gartner, A. (1996a). Questions most asked: What research says about inclusion. *Impact on Instructional Improvement, 25*(1), 77–82.

Lipsky & Gartner. (1996b). Inclusive education and school restructuring. In W. Stainback & S. Stainback (Eds.). *Controversial issues confronting special education.* Needham Heights, MA: Allyn and Bacon.

Oberti v. Board of Education, 995 F. 2d 1204, 19 IDELR 908 (3rd Cir., 1993).

Peterson, M., & Beloin, K. (1998). Teaching the inclusive teacher. *Teacher Education and Special Education, Vol. 21, #4*, pp. 306–318.

Sacramento City School Dist. v. Rachel H., 14 F. 3d 1398 (9th Cir., 1994).

Sapon-Shevin, M. (1992). Celebrating diversity, creating community. In W. Stainback & S. Stainback (Eds.). *Curriculum considerations in inclusive classrooms.* Baltimore: Paul H. Brookes.

Shaffner, B., & Busewell, B. (1996). Ten critical elements for creating inclusive and effective school communities. In W. Stainback & S. Stainback (Eds.). *Inclusion: A guide for educators*. Baltimore: Paul H. Brookes.

Scruggs, T. E., & Mastropieri, M. A. (1996). Teacher perceptions of mainstreaming/inclusion, 1958–1995: A research synthesis. *Exceptional Children, 63*, 59–74.

Villa, R., & Thousand, J. (1992). Student collaboration: An essential for curriculum delivery in the 21st century. In W. Stainback & S. Stainback (Eds.). *Curriculum considerations in inclusive classrooms*. Baltimore: Paul H. Brookes.

Appendix

A

Definitions
of Disabilities

Definitions of disabilities defined in the Individuals with Disabilities Education Act

§300.7 Child with a disability.

(a) **General.**

(1) As used in this part, the term **child with a disability** means a child evaluated in accordance with §§300.530–300.536 as having mental retardation, a hearing impairment including deafness, a speech or language impairment, a visual impairment including blindness, serious emotional disturbance (hereafter referred to as emotional disturbance), an orthopedic impairment, autism, traumatic brain injury, another health impairment, a specific learning disability, deaf-blindness, or multiple disabilities, and who, by reason thereof, needs special education and related services.

(2)

(i) Subject to paragraph (a)(2)(ii) of this section, if it is determined, through an appropriate evaluation under §§300.530–300.536, that a child has one of the disabilities identified in paragraph (a)(1) of this section, but only needs a related service and not special education, the child is not a **child with a disability** under this part.

(ii) If, consistent with §300.26(a)(2), the related service required by the child is considered special education rather than a related service under State standards, the child would be determined to be a **child with a disability** under paragraph (a)(1) of this section.

(b) **Children aged 3 through 9 experiencing developmental delays.** The term **child with a disability** for children aged 3 through 9 may, at the discretion of the State and LEA and in accordance with §300.313, include a child:

(1) Who is experiencing developmental delays, as defined by the State and as measured by appropriate diagnostic instruments and procedures, in one or more of the following areas: physical development, cognitive development, communication development, social or emotional development, or adaptive development; and

(2) Who, by reason thereof, needs special education and related services.

(c) **Definitions of disability terms.** The terms used in this definition are defined as follows:

(1)

(i) **Autism** means a developmental disability significantly affecting verbal and nonverbal communication and social interaction, generally evident before age 3, that adversely affects a child's educational performance. Other characteristics often associated with autism are engagement in repetitive activities and stereotyped movements, resistance to environmental change or change in daily routines, and unusual responses to sensory experiences. The term does not apply if a child's educational performance is adversely affected primarily because the child has an emotional disturbance, as defined in paragraph (c)(4) of this section.

(ii) A child who manifests the characteristics of "autism" after age 3 could be diagnosed as having "autism" if the criteria in paragraph (c)(1)(i) of this section are satisfied.

(2) **Deaf-blindness** means concomitant hearing and visual impairments, the combination of which causes such severe communication and other developmental and educational needs that they cannot be accommodated in special education programs solely for children with deafness or children with blindness.

(3) **Deafness** means a hearing impairment that is so severe that the child is impaired in processing linguistic information through hearing, with or without amplification, that adversely affects a child's educational performance.

(4) **Emotional disturbance** is defined as follows:

(i) The term means a condition exhibiting one or more of the following characteristics over a long period of time and to a marked degree that adversely affects a child's educational performance:

(a) An inability to learn that cannot be explained by intellectual, sensory, or health factors.

(b) An inability to build or maintain satisfactory interpersonal relationships with peers and teachers.

(c) Inappropriate types of behavior or feelings under normal circumstances.

(d) A general pervasive mood of unhappiness or depression.

(e) A tendency to develop physical symptoms or fears associated with personal or school problems.

(ii) The term includes schizophrenia. The term does not apply to children who are socially maladjusted, unless it is determined that they have an emotional disturbance.

(5) **Hearing impairment** means an impairment in hearing, whether permanent or fluctuating, that adversely affects a child's educational performance but that is not included under the definition of deafness in this section.

(6) **Mental retardation** means significantly subaverage general intellectual functioning, existing concurrently with deficits in adaptive behavior and manifested during the developmental period, that adversely affects a child's educational performance.

(7) **Multiple disabilities** means concomitant impairments (such as mental retardation-blindness, mental retardation-orthopedic impairment, etc.), the combination of which causes such severe educational needs that they cannot be accommodated in special education programs solely for one of the impairments. The term does not include deaf-blindness.

(8) **Orthopedic impairment** means a severe orthopedic impairment that adversely affects a child's educational performance. The term includes impairments caused by congenital anomaly (e.g., clubfoot, absence of some member, etc.), impairments caused by disease (e.g., poliomyelitis, bone tuberculosis, etc.), and impairments from other causes (e.g., cerebral palsy, amputations, and fractures or burns that cause contractures).

(9) **Other health impairment** means having limited strength, vitality, or alertness, including a heightened alertness to environmental stimuli, that results in limited alertness with respect to the educational environment, that:

(i) is due to chronic or acute health problems, such as asthma, attention deficit disorder or attention deficit hyperactivity disorder, diabetes, epilepsy, a heart condition, hemophilia, lead poisoning, leukemia, nephritis, rheumatic fever, and sickle cell anemia; and

(ii) adversely affects a child's educational performance.

(10) **Specific learning disability** is defined as follows:

(i) **General.** The term means a disorder in one or more of the basic psychological processes involved in understanding or in using language, spoken or written, that may manifest itself in an imperfect ability to listen, think, speak, read, write, spell, or to do mathematical calculations, including conditions such as perceptual disabilities, brain injury, minimal brain dysfunction, dyslexia, and developmental aphasia.

(ii) **Disorders not included.** The term does not include learning problems that are primarily the result of visual, hearing, or motor disabilities, of mental retardation, of emotional disturbance, or of environmental, cultural, or economic disadvantage.

(11) **Speech or language impairment** means a communication disorder, such as stuttering, impaired articulation, a language impairment, or a voice impairment, that adversely affects a child's educational performance.

(12) **Traumatic brain injury** means an acquired injury to the brain caused by an external physical force, resulting in total or partial functional disability or psychosocial impairment, or both, that adversely affects a child's educational performance. The term applies to open or closed head injuries resulting in impairments in one or more areas, such as cognition, language, memory, attention, reasoning, abstract thinking, judgment, problem solving, sensory, perceptual, and motor abilities, psychosocial behavior, physical functions, information processing, and speech. The term does not apply to brain injuries that are congenital or degenerative, or to brain injuries induced by birth trauma.

(13) **Visual impairment including blindness** means an impairment in vision that, even with correction, adversely affects a child's educational performance. The term includes both partial sight and blindness.

The above is adapted from:

Individuals with Disabilities Education Act, 20 U.S.C. 1400 et seq. (1997).

Strategies
to Support Inclusion

*The following list is a compilation of strategies for teachers to consider when working with students with disabilities. It should not be assumed that, for some students, giving them study guides, graphic organizers, outlines, or various tools is sufficient. Students may also need instruction on **how to use** these tools.*

General

- Preteach vocabulary
- Preview major concepts
- Provide for repetition of instruction
- Group work where they can discuss key concepts
- Provide examples and allow student to apply to personal experiences
- Provide a study guide and have student highlight key points as you discuss them
- Incorporate verbal presentation with written work, board work, hands-on activities (Chalmers, 1992)
- Make time adjustments for students who need more time to process and apply information
- Provide feedback—let students know why their grade is what it is and how they can improve
- Provide alternate assignments (see section on multiple intelligences in chapter 4)
- Use multiple choice, matching, short answer tests when possible

Organizational

- Require students to keep an assignment notebook. Periodically, check those of students with disabilities to ensure they know how to use it, and that they *are* using it.
- Provide written checklists of tasks to be completed
- Color-code materials for each class/subject
- Written cues for how to organize—"First, you do this,…"

Science and social studies

- Chooses textbooks carefully. Ensure the language is clear. Is it well organized? Does it present a clear organizational framework with headings, summaries, lists, and graphic organizers? Are pictures and graphs easy to read?
- Help the students to understand how to use the text, e.g., how the topic sentences, lists, organizational charts, etc. can help them learn the material
- Use visual aids, graphic organizers, charts to help the students study and understand the relationship of concepts to each other.
- Use study guides. Have the students who can develop their own, perhaps with a peer. Leave room on the guides for students to take notes.
- Give students reasons to read the material. E.g., "Let's find out how erosion happens. Read pp. 234–235 and find the answer."
- Promote students' memory using strategies such as rehearsal of key facts, categorization or clustering of concepts, chunking of smaller pieces of material, mnemonics strategies, visualization, key word memorization (Salend, 1998)
- Integrate areas of the curriculum whenever possible. Providing students with an art or math activity, for example, that relates to science or social studies helps to reinforce and extend their understanding of the content.
- Provide assistance for students in writing term papers. They will need the organizational strategies to plan their paper and frequent feedback and assistance in the writing of the paper.

Mathematics

- Use of graph paper to line up numbers of equations
- Use of calculator to solve problems or check work. There are calculators that do graphing, rounding to the nearest dollar, etc.
- Use manipulatives to solve problems. Some students can solve the problems with pencil and paper and others need objects. Unifix cubes, milk bottle caps, etc. can be used.

- Use of number line to complete addition and subtraction problems
- Use lined paper vertically for columns and for numbers to line up equations
- Flashcards for drill for basic facts
- Multiplication chart
- Problem-solving grid to dissect the problem, asking for key words, operations needed, hidden numbers, etc.
- Allow students to draw pictures to represent the problem
- Fraction kits for solving equations. These can be in the shapes of circles or rectangles and made from a variety of mediums.
- Fraction bars for learning fraction equivalents. Strips of 11 x 14 in construction paper with number on them that can be aligned to show equivalent fractions. For example, one bar may have the numbers 1–9 and another may have the numbers 2, 4, 6, 8, 10, 12, 14, 16, 18. When aligned, student will see fractions that are equivalent to 1/2.
- Preteach mathematics vocabulary
- Bridging to ten, i.e., $7 + 5 = ?$, $7 + 3 + 10$ and 2 more equals 12
- Counting on, starting with the largest number and counting from there, i.e., $7 + ? = 13$. Starting at seven, one would count on until 13.
- Near doubles, i.e., $8 + 9 = ?$, $8 + 8 + 16$ and 1 more is 17
- Problem-solving ROSE (read the question, organize the facts, select the operation and solve, evaluate the answer)
- Give fewer problems to solve
- Provide key with mathematics symbols and meanings

Reading

- Provide books on tapes
- Have students read in pairs
- Choral reading
- Assign less reading
- Use high-interest, low-difficulty (HILD) books
- Use reading template to highlight sentences. These are cardboard strips with a window, the size of a sentence cut out that students can move down as they read.
- Use graphic organizers (story grammar, story maps, character maps, venn diagrams, etc.)
- Preteach vocabulary
- Reread

- Questioning by either student or teacher. Teacher can ask specific questions for students to answer when reading, i.e., How did the character change, and what influenced the character?, and students can ask themselves questions when reading, i.e., How will they solve the problem?
- Predicting what will happen next and confirming predictions
- Activate prior knowledge through discussion, real life experiences, and/or videos
- Color-code important words with highlight tape
- Guided reading groups
- Language Experience Approach—writing about what the students have experienced and then reading it, i.e., a field trip is taken, students write about the experience individually or as a group and then read what is written
- Use cloze procedure—a fill-in-the-blank activity
- Flashcards for high-frequency word practice
- Allow more time

Writing

- Reduce amount of writing
- Use graphic organizers (paragraph starters, story frames, venn diagram, etc.)
- Use large pencils
- Use the computer
- Use AlphaSmart keyboard
- Language Experience Approach (see above)
- Provide outline of notes with key words missing
- Allow peer to take notes using carbon paper
- Pencil grips
- Personal dictionaries
- Dictate writing to be typed out by "peer secretary"
- Oral presentations rather than written assignments
- Story openers, provide list of openers for stories to get student started
- Models of finished product
- Conferencing with students about writing
- Sentence cube Scrabble™ for practice with sentence structure
- Editing checklists
- Allow more time

The previous information is adapted from:

Chalmers, L. (1992). *Modifying curriculum for special needs students in the regular classroom.* Moorhead, MN: Practical Press.

Choate, J. S. (2000). *Successful inclusive teaching: Proven ways to detect and correct special needs.* Boston: Allyn and Bacon.

Hatfield, M. M., Edwards, N. T., Bitter, G. G., & Morrow, J. (2003). *Mathematics methods for elementary and middle school teachers.* New York: John Wiley & Sons.

Salend, S. (1998). *Effective mainstreaming: Creating inclusive classrooms.* Upper Saddle River, NJ: Merrill.

Homework

- Remind students of due dates periodically
- Coordinate with other teachers to prevent homework overload
- Establish a routine at the beginning of the year for how homework will be assigned
- Assign homework toward the beginning of class
- Write the assignment on the board and leave it there until the assignment is due
- Relate homework to classwork or real life (and/or inform students how they will use the content of the homework in real life)
- Explain how to do the homework, provide examples, and write directions on the chalkboard
- Have students begin the homework in class, check that they understand, and provide assistance as necessary
- Allow students to work together on homework
- Make sure students and parents have information regarding the policy on missed and late assignments, extra credit, and available adaptations. Establish a set routine at the beginning of the year.
- Assign work that the students can do
- Assign homework in small units
- Explain the assignment clearly

The above is adapted from:

Warger, C. (2001). *Five homework strategies for teaching students with disabilities.* Retrieved January 4, 2002, from The ERIC Clearinghouse on Disabilities and Gifted Education (ERIC EC) http://ericec.org/digests/e608.html.

Sample 504 Plan

Section 504
Student Accommodation Plan

Name _____ Birthdate _____ Plan Date_____
Address _____Phone_____
School _____ Grade_____

Parent(s) Name _____
Parent Address _____

Student's Disability _____
Describe the basis for the determination of the disability_____
_____
_____

Major Life Activity(ies) Affected: _____
_____
_____

Reasonable Accommodations/Services (Check any interventions which directly apply to student's area of difficulty. Additional interventions may be found in district's accommodation suggestion list.)

Physical	Organizational	Curricular	Behavioral
❏ preferential seating	❏ self-monitoring strategies	❏ hands-on materials and activities	❏ private signals
❏ adjust class schedule	❏ increase time for tests	❏ give examples	❏ individualized support plan
❏ carpet on classroom floors	❏ highlight main ideas in text	❏ offer alternative assignments	❏ positive verbal and/or written feedback
❏ allow increased student movement	❏ structured assignment notebook	❏ provide written directions	❏ student contracts
❏	❏	❏	❏

Date for Review/Reassessment _____

_____   _____
Signature of Parent, Guardian, or Student (if 18 years or older)   Date

_____   _____
Signature of 504 Liaison   Date

_____   _____
Signature of Principal   Date

Section 504
Student Accommodation Plan

Name _____ Birthdate _____ Plan Date_____
Address _____Phone_____
School _____ Grade_____

Parent(s) Name _____
Parent Address _____

Student's Disability _____
Major Life Activity(ies) Affected by Disability (explain) _____
_____
_____

Reasonable Accommodations/Services (specify):
A. Physical Accommodations (if any)_____
_____
_____

B. Instructional Accommodations (if any) _____
_____
_____

C. Related aids and services (if any) _____
_____
_____

D. Other (if any, please be specific) _____
_____
_____

Date for Review/Reassessment _____

_____   _____
Signature of Parent, Guardian, or Student (if 18 years or older)   Date

_____   _____
Signature of 504 Liaison   Date

_____   _____
Signature of Principal   Date

Index

Accommodations. *See also Paulson & Fognani-Smaus.*
  and curriculum, 44–45
  defined, 44
  examples, 44
Activity/skills matrix
  illustration of, 48
  as a self-monitoring device, 49
  and student goals, 47–49, 60
  and vocational skills, 53
Age-appropriate peers
  and the general education classroom, 8
  natural occurrence of, 8
  and optimal environment for students with disabilities, 8
  as role models for students with disabilities, 9, 47
Americans with Disabilities Act (ADA). *See also Rehabilitation Act (Section 504).*
  effects of implementation of, 7
  as extension of Rehabilitation Act (Section 504), 91
  teacher knowledge of, 96–97

Baker, Wang, & Walberg
  on effectiveness of general education placements, 12
Bartlett, Weisenstein, & Etscheidt
  realities on inclusion cited by, 95
Barton & Landman
  importance of inclusion as a social issue, 16
Blazer, B.
  development of accommodation plans for teachers, 91

Brown et al.
  inclusion and student interaction, 9, 13
Brown v. the Board of Education
  basis of, 6, 31
  and inclusion, 95
  influence of on students with disabilities, 6

CAST Universal Design for Learning (UDL)
  as a new approach to teaching, 73–74
  premise of, 73
Cloze procedure. *See also Differentiated Instruction.*
  defined, 61
  and reading, 116

Dev & Scruggs
  inclusion and positive teacher attitudes, 98
Differentiated instruction. *See also Tomlinson, C. A.*
  assumptions of, 61–62
  defined, 61
  examples of, 63, 65, 68
  and teachers, 62
Direct Instruction
  specialized programs of, 74
    Orton-Gillingham, 74
    Touch Math, 74
    Wilson Reading, 74
  as a teaching approach, 74
Dyscalculia. *See also Differentiated Instruction.*
  defined, 67

About the Authors

Elaine Francis

Elaine Francis is a professor of special education at Fitchburg State College in Fitchburg, Massachusetts. She has been a special educator for the past three decades. She serves as a consultant to various school districts on inclusionary practices for elementary through post-secondary levels. Most recently her work has focused on the preparation of paraprofessionals to work with students with disabilities, and to ultimately become teachers. In addition to teaching and consulting, she has presented at national conferences on topics such as evaluation and enhancement of teacher preparation programs to meet the changing demands of today's schools.

Ruth M. Joseph

Ruth Joseph is an assistant professor in the Education Department at Lasell College in Newton, Massachusetts. After 12 years in special education, Ruth now teaches reading and writing instruction and assessment. In addition to college teaching, Ruth works as a reading consultant to various school districts. She has presented at national and international conferences on topics in special education, reading, and technology in general and special education teacher education programs.

Anne M. Howard

Anne Howard is a professor of special education at Fitchburg State College in Fitchburg, Massachusetts. She coordinates the graduate licensure program in severe disabilities, and has served as the Director of the Faculty Center for Teaching Excellence. In addition to her work at Fitchburg State College, Anne devotes her time and expertise consulting to various school districts on special education policies and programs. She frequently provides support in the area of functional behavior assessment and the integration of related services. Anne also serves on the Board of Directors for the Federation for Children with Special Needs.